Passport's Illustrated Guide to

IRELAND

THIRD EDITION

GW00702824

PASSPORT BOOKS

NTC/Contemporary Publishing Group

This edition first published in 2000 by Passport Books
A division of NTC/Contemporary Publishing Group, Inc.
4255 West Touhy Avenue
Lincolnwood (Chicago), Illinois
60712–1975 U.S.A.

Written by Eric and Ruth Bailey

© The Automobile Association 1994, 1999, 2000
Maps © The Automobile Association 1994, 1999, 2000

ISBN 0-658-00504-9

Town plans (Republic of Ireland) reproduced by permission of the Director of Ordnance Survey Ireland © Government of Ireland 1999 (Permit No. 6885).
Town plans (Northern Ireland) reproduced by permission of the Director and Chief Executive, Ordnance Survey of Northern Ireland, acting on behalf of the Controller of Her Majesty's Stationery Office © Crown copyright 1999 (Permit No. 1322).

The contents of this publication are believed correct at the time of printing. Nevertheless, the publishers cannot be held responsible for any errors or omissions, or for changes in the details given in this guide, or for the consequences of any reliance on the information provided by the same. Assessments of attractions, hotels, restaurants, and so forth are based upon the author's own experience and, therefore, descriptions given in this guide necessarily contain an element of subjective opinion that may not reflect the publishers' opinions or dictate a reader's own experiences on another occasion.
We have tried to ensure accuracy in this guide, but things do change and we would be grateful if readers would advise us of any inaccuracies they may encounter.

Published by Passport Books in conjunction with AA Publishing and the Thomas Cook Group Ltd.

Color separation: BTB Colour Reproduction, Whitchurch, Hampshire, England

Printed by Edicoes ASA, Oporto, Portugal

Cover photographs: front, copyright © Dave G. Houser; spine, © Steve Bly/Dave G. Houser Stock Photography.

Contents

About this Book

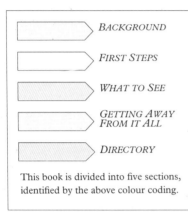

BACKGROUND

FIRST STEPS

WHAT TO SEE

GETTING AWAY
FROM IT ALL

DIRECTORY

This book is divided into five sections, identified by the above colour coding.

TELEPHONE NUMBERS
If you have difficulty in reaching any of the telephone numbers in this book, dial 1190 (Republic of Ireland) or 192 (N Ireland) for assistance.

Background gives an introduction to the country – its history, geography, politics, culture.
First Steps offers practical advice on arriving and getting around.
What to See is an alphabetical listing of places to visit, divided into four regions, interspersed with walks and tours.
Getting Away From it All highlights places off the beaten track where it's possible to relax and enjoy peace and quiet.
Finally, the **Directory** provides practical information – from shopping and entertainment to children and sport, including a section on business matters. Special highly illustrated features on specific aspects of the country appear throughout the book.

Ireland's landscape of broad plains and gently rolling green hills

BACKGROUND

'I am beginning to find out now, that a man ought to be forty years in the country instead of three months, and then he wouldn't be able to write about it. I wonder who does understand the place?'

WILLIAM THACKERAY,
Letter to Mrs Carmichael-Smyth (1842)

Introduction

*I*reland means different things to different people, but some things are common to everyone. Everybody remarks on the natural and sincere warmth of the welcome they get from the Irish people. Nobody can fail to appreciate the landscapes and seascapes – sometimes spectacular and wild, sometimes beautiful, other times merely pretty.

The early Christian and prehistoric megaliths, dolmens, round towers and ruins are awe-inspiring, often mysterious. Coming across them casually, sometimes unexpectedly, both in the town and the countryside evokes a profound sense of antiquity.

Another thing that cannot go unnoticed in Ireland is that the elements rarely keep still for long. You could stand in one spot watching the changing scene. Blue sky, contrasting sunlight and shadow. Two minutes later, banking clouds, sun in and out. After that, grey streaks the sky – reach for your umbrella. The grey thickens into rolling swaths, almost navy blue, then out comes the sun, with a rainbow, or two, for company. The landscape responds to the fickle weather, bright or hazy, picked out in distant detail, suddenly brooding.

Dublin is a flirtatious city, captivating its visitors. Belfast has dignity. Wexford, Waterford, Cork – all have their own distinctive character. And everywhere the seafood is sublime. Most visitors appreciate the social life, which takes place to a large extent in the many

Rolling moorlands in the Wicklow Mountains

IRELAND – COUNTIES AND REGIONS

Dublin & Leinster

Munster

Connacht

Ulster

Donegal
Lifford

Londonderry

Antrim

NORTHERN
IRELAND ■ Belfast

Tyrone

Sligo
Sligo

Leitrim

Fermanagh

Armagh Down

Monaghan
Monaghan

Dundalk

Mayo

Castlebar

Carrick-on-
Shannon

Cavan
Cavan

Louth

Roscommon
Roscommon

Longford
Longford

Navan

Galway

Mullingar
West Meath

Meath

Dublin
■ Dublin

Galway

Offaly

Tullamore

Naas

Kildare

REPUBLIC OF
IRELAND

Clare

Ennis

Portlaoise

Laois

Wicklow

Wicklow

Carlow

Tipperary
Kilkenny

Carlow

Limerick
Limerick

Kilkenny
Kilkenny

Wexford

Tralee

Clonmel

Wexford

Waterford Waterford

Kerry

Cork

Cork

| 0 | 50 | 100 km |
| 0 | | 50 miles |

friendly pubs and bars.

But Ireland is essentially rural. There is rarely too much traffic for the roads and if you come to a hold-up it will probably be cows crossing for milking, or sheep moving to fresh pastures.

History

About 6000BC
Mesolithic settlers cross to northeast·
Ireland from the west coast of Scotland.
About 3000BC
Neolithic immigrants introduce
agriculture, weaving and pottery and
begin building huge megaliths.
About 600BC
Celts arrive from Britain and France;
Ireland is divided into provinces.
About AD350
Christianity arrives in Ireland.
432
St Patrick arrives.
795
Full-scale invasion by the Vikings.
1014
High King Brian Ború defeats the
Vikings at Clontarf, but his murder
prevents unification of Ireland.
1169
The Anglo-Norman 'Strongbow' helps
Dermot MacMurrough, deposed King
of Leinster, to regain his throne.
1172
England's Henry II is made overlord of
Ireland, opening the way for the
establishment of Anglo-Norman estates.
1366
The Statutes of Kilkenny forbid inter-
marriage with the Irish, who are also
banned from cities, and makes the
adoption of Irish names, customs and
language illegal.
1534–40
Lord Offaly stages an insurrection after
Henry VIII breaks with the Catholic
Church; Offaly and five brothers are
executed when the insurrection fails.
1541
Henry VIII forces Irish chiefs to
surrender their lands.

1558–1603
Elizabeth I tightens English hold on
Ireland and launches the 'Plantation'
policy, establishing English and Scottish
settlers on land seized from the Irish.
1595–1603
Hugh O'Neill, Earl of Tyrone, leads a
rebellion, but has to surrender.
1607
O'Neill leads other chiefs in the 'Flight
of the Earls' to Europe.
1641
Belief that Charles I of England is a
Catholic sympathiser provokes rebellion
in Ulster and Civil War in England.
1649
Oliver Cromwell invades Ireland after
defeating and executing Charles I;
thousands of Irish are massacred.
1653
Under the Act of Settlement, Cromwell's
opponents have their lands seized.
1689–90
King James II of England flees to
Ireland after being deposed. He is
defeated by William III at the Battle of
the Boyne.
1704
The first of a number of laws to be
known as the Penal Code restrict
Catholic land-owning and subsequently
ban Catholics from voting, attending
schools and military service.
1775
The American War of Independence
promotes unrest in Ireland.
1782
Grattan's Parliament – named after
Henry Grattan – persuades the British
government that the time has come for
Catholic emancipation and Irish
independence, but nothing comes of it.

1798
United Irishmen, led by Wolfe Tone, stage an uprising which is crushed.
1800
Ireland becomes part of Britain under the Act of Union.
1829
The Catholic Emancipation Act is passed after Daniel O'Connell, 'The Liberator', gains a seat at Westminster.
1845–8
Ireland's population is reduced by some 2 million as a result of starvation due to potato crop failures and emigration.
1881
Charles Stewart Parnell, Home Rule Party leader, encourages the Irish to defy difficult landlords.
1905–8
The Sinn Fein party is founded after the defeat of two Home Rule bills.
1914
Implementation of Home Rule is post-poned because of the outbreak of war.
1916
The Irish Republican Brotherhood stages insurrection in Dublin – the Easter Rising. When the rebellion fails 16 of its leaders are executed.
1920–1
Fighting breaks out between Britain and Ireland; the Anglo-Irish Treaty creates the Irish Free State and allows six counties to remain part of Britain.
1922
Republicans reject the Treaty. Cvil war ensues, ending when Fianna Fáil party founder, Eamonn De Valera, is arrested.
1932
De Valera is elected President of the Irish Free State.
1949
The Republic of Ireland is created.
1969
Rioting between Catholics and

Protestants at the Apprentice Boys' March in Londonderry. British troops arrive as peacekeepers. The Provisional IRA launches a campaign of violence.
1972
Thirteen unarmed demonstrators are shot by British troops on 30 January – 'Bloody Sunday'. Stormont is suspended and Westminster imposes direct rule. Severe emergency laws are enforced as acts of terrorism by both sides continue.
1986
Under the Anglo-Irish Agreement, the Republic has more say in Northern affairs.
1994
IRA and Loyalist paramilitary announce ceasefire nine months after signing of Downing Street Declaration by Britain and Ireland.
1998
The Good Friday Peace Agreement is signed by all sides. Talks continue in the hope of finding a peaceful solution.

Parnell, 19th-century nationalist leader

EARLY HISTORY

Prehistory lives on in Ireland today. A prolific heritage of field monuments – stone circles, dolmens, passage graves and Celtic forts – dating from thousands of years BC, provides a source of wonder and meditation. They can be found almost everywhere. Many are signposted, and the visitor casually encounters unspoilt ancient monuments which most countries would greedily exploit.

Visiting some of them may involve a walk through muddy farmland. Such is the case of the pagan Janus figure, a squat Celtic idol facing both ways in a tiny Fermanagh graveyard on Boa Island. Others, like the great Newgrange tumulus in Co Meath, are easily accessible and present a sophisticated approach to tourism.

Ancient religious monuments dedicated to the old gods, pagan fertility symbols, final resting places, primitive calendars – the purpose for which these monuments were constructed is often a matter of academic debate.

One of the country's most interesting surviving mounds is at the Hill of Tara, in Co Meath. Originally including a hill fort and several ring forts, it was the residence of the High Kings of Ireland over many centuries.

Left: carved figures on White Island combine Christian and pagan features

Left: the two-faced, stone-carved Janus figure in Caldragh churchyard, Boa Island, exerts a brooding fascination

Above: Kilnaraune pillar stone, engraved with symbolic scenes

Left: entrance to Bronze Age Newgrange tomb

Visitors can see the entrance to a passage grave where finds included the cremated remains of 40 people, and various utensils, which have been carbon-dated at 1800BC. Also found was the skeleton of a teenage boy wearing a necklace of amber, jet and bronze. His was the only body not cremated.

Celtic crosses, or high crosses, usually very decorative, stand proudly in churchyards throughout Ireland, dating from the early 12th century onwards, some depicting scenes from the scriptures.

Geography

*I*reland lies on the continental shelf to the west of the European mainland. On the east it is separated from Britain by the Irish Sea. To the northeast, the North Channel brings Scotland to within 21km of the Antrim coast. To the west lies the vastness of the Atlantic Ocean, while to the south St George's Channel separates Ireland from France.

Two great mountain ranges converge in Ireland. The older Caledonian system extending from Scandinavia and Scotland to the north and west of Ireland, gives rise to the rugged terrain of Counties Donegal, Galway and Mayo. The younger Armorican system extends from central Europe through Brittany to southwest Ireland, culminating in 1,041m-high Carrauntoohill, the country's highest mountain, in Macgillycuddy's Reeks. Killarney's celebrated 'lakes and fells' are on the eastern slopes of the Reeks.

A narrow belt of lowland crosses the country from the Carlingford Peninsula and the Wicklow Mountains in the east to the Atlantic Ocean in the west, along the Shannon Estuary, Galway Bay, Clew Bay and Donegal Bay. In Co Clare, the lowland rises westward, terminating at the magnificent Cliffs of Moher.

The stately 340km-long River Shannon is the largest of Ireland's rivers. Rising in Co Leitrim, it opens up into a series of attractive lakes before reaching its broad, indented estuary between Counties Clare and Limerick.

The main eastward-flowing rivers are the Lagan, which runs to the sea at Belfast; the Liffey, with Dublin at its mouth; and the Slaney, which meets the sea at Wexford. In Ulster, the River Erne flows north, opening into Upper and Lower Lough Erne before entering Donegal Bay.

Ireland's climate is legendary, and there is some truth in the joke that observes: 'When you can see the mountain it means it is going to rain; when you cannot see it, it is raining.' In reality, though, the climate is mild and without extremes, due largely to the Gulf Stream, whose relatively warm waters wash Ireland's shores.

The heaviest rainfall is in Donegal,

The Giant's Causeway – 40,000 hexagonal basalt columns formed by volcanic rock as it cooled, 60 million years ago

Kerry and Mayo, where it may exceed 3,000mm. Eastern Ireland is much drier, with Dublin averaging only 785mm a year.

Two bonuses, however, arise from Ireland's variable weather: the constantly changing light and verdant vegetation. Though limited, the flora has many interesting features. The lanes of Cork and Kerry, for example, are noted for their profuse fuchsia hedgerows, while an Arctic-Alpine flora thrives in the Burren in Co Clare.

Among Ireland's 27 mammal species are red deer, pine martens, badgers, hares, otters and stoats. The only reptile is the common lizard. Rivers and lakes are rich in salmon, trout and char, as well as coarse fish. Around 125 species of wild birds breed in the island and more than 250 visiting species have been recorded.

The meandering valley of Glenmacnass in the Wicklow Mountains

THOMAS COOK'S IRELAND

After organising an excursion to Liverpool in 1846, Thomas Cook set off for Ireland in 1853. Following some difficulty in obtaining facilities from railway managers, a series of tours was set up by John Mason Cook, Thomas Cook's son.

An office was established in Dublin in 1874, and by the end of the century a special brochure advertised tours to every part of Ireland. At that time there were offices in Dublin, Belfast, Queenstown and Cork.

During World War II the Belfast office remained open and was heavily involved in the movement of Allied troops.

Politics

*F*or outsiders, one issue dominates all Irish politics – 'the Troubles'. While it is true that serious political unrest continues, the majority of people – north and south of the border – lead peaceful lives and are able to focus on normal domestic political issues.

However, even though the easy-going Irish can – and do – talk about any subject under the sun, politics, while not taboo, is a topic best avoided by visitors. This advice, which also embraces religion, is frequently meted out to people travelling anywhere in the world, but is particularly applied to Ireland, because even the most reasonable character can get hot under the collar when a stranger talks Irish politics in a less-than-knowledgeable way.

Politicians from the Republic, Northern Ireland and the UK have tried many times to find ways to stop 'the Troubles'. The 1994 ceasefire which followed the signing of the Downing Street Declaration in 1993 floundered with the IRA's bombing of Canary Wharf in London in 1996. Progress towards a final solution is slow and old attitudes on all sides die hard.

The facts outlined here may provide a little background to the current situation.

Ireland has been politically divided since 1920–1. After centuries of British rule, including a 120-year period when the whole of Ireland was governed as

Neo-classical Stormont – the former Northern Ireland Parliament building, Belfast

part of the United Kingdom, 26 of its 32 counties gained their independence.

Six stayed out, forming Northern Ireland and remaining in the United Kingdom. They are Antrim, Armagh, Londonderry, Down, Fermanagh and Tyrone, in the Province of Ulster. The other counties of Ulster – Cavan, Donegal and Monaghan – are in the Republic of Ireland. The Constitution of Ireland and the Republic of Ireland Act (1949) severed Ireland's last formal links with Britain.

Northern Ireland elects 17 MPs to Parliament at Westminster. From 1921 to 1972, although Northern Ireland was represented at Westminster, the devolved Government at Stormont operated with virtual autonomy from London on local matters.

In 1972, as a result of increased IRA activity in Northern Ireland and paramilitary action by so-called Loyalist extremist groups, the British Government resumed direct responsibility for all aspects of the government of Northern Ireland. The Secretary of State for Northern Ireland is a member of the British Cabinet.

The Government of the Republic is a parliamentary democracy, with two Houses of Parliament – the Dáil, or House of Representatives, and the Seanad (Senate). The President is the head of state, and the Prime Minister (Taoiseach) is head of the Government. Where there is more than one candidate for the presidency, the President is elected by direct vote of the people.

The Constitution of Ireland, adopted by referendum in 1937, sets out the form of government, defining its powers and those of the President and Prime Minister. It also defines the structure and powers of the courts, sets out the

Leinster House is the seat of the Dáil (House of Representatives) and the Seanad (Senate)

fundamental rights of citizens and contains a number of directive principles of social policy.

The Dáil currently has 166 members, with six main political parties represented – Fianna Fáil, Fine Gael, Labour, Progressive Democrats, Democratic Left and the Workers' Party. The Seanad, with 60 members, may initiate or amend legislation.

Under the Constitution every citizen has the right to petition the courts to secure his or her rights or to have a judgement pronounced as to whether given legislation is compatible with the Constitution. Before signing a bill, the President may refer it to the Supreme Court for a decision on its compatibility with the Constitution. This procedure has led to a number of laws or parts of laws being declared unconstitutional and therefore void.

Local government, responsible for public housing, water and sanitation, road maintenance, vocational education and other services, is administered by 113 local authorities funded by state grants and local taxes on non-residential property.

Culture

*I*rish culture is a mystic blend of past and present, and the borders between myth and reality, magic and technology, absurdity and order are blurred. Legend merges into history, and myth becomes more tangible with the realisation that the places of legend actually exist.

Ireland's roots are firmly embedded in Celtic soil. The Celts, initially migrants, were an independent, imaginative people who loved a good song, a good story, a good argument and a good fight. Were? You will find them today – as proud of their heritage among the chic boutiques of Dublin's Grafton Street as they are on the windswept moorlands of Kerry and Connemara.

The Celtic character has survived the violent prejudice of centuries. Oppression by the English, especially the 18th-century Penal Laws, stifled Irish culture and the Irish language almost to the point of extinction. Almost, but not quite.

Clandestine 'hedgerow schools' were set up, and when Ireland eventually became fully independent, Irish (Gaelic) was adopted as the first national language. It is now a compulsory subject in schools and is more widely spoken than at any time since the 19th century.

A major part of Britain's efforts to subjugate the Irish was the policy of 'plantation', under which Protestant migrants from England and Scotland were settled on lands confiscated from native Irish Catholics. Descendants of the Anglo-Irish Ascendancy, the privileged elite who controlled Ireland, still hold estates in the Republic. Caught between two worlds – an Irish homeland and an English heritage – they are treated with polite caution by their Irish neighbours, who still regard them as more English than the English.

Today, the Irish have regained a sense of identity that was almost lost forever, and Celtic pride is reflected in the traditional lettering on high street shop fronts, in literature, the arts and music.

Signposts display names in both English and Irish, particularly in the Republic

FIRST STEPS

'Ireland is a little Russia in
which the
longest way round is the
shortest way home,
and the means more
important than the end.'
GEORGE MOORE,
Ave (1911)

ARRIVING
By air

There are five major international airports in Ireland: Shannon, Dublin, Cork, Knock and Belfast International at Aldergrove.

Shannon is the gateway for flights from North America (there are also flights to Dublin from the US), but airline options for scheduled services are limited to Ireland's national carrier, Aer Lingus, Continental Airlines and Delta. Flying via London offers more choice for travellers from Canada and the US.

Dublin Airport has good European connections. Aer Lingus, British Airways, British Midland and Ryanair are the main carriers on routes between the UK and Ireland, while Aer Lingus and other major national airlines serve major European cities.

Cork Airport has direct flights to Dublin, London and limited continental destinations, with good connecting international flights through Dublin.

Knock International Airport, Charlestown, Co Mayo, owes its existence to a local priest, who campaigned for years for an airport to serve the pilgrims who flock to the village where apparitions of the Virgin Mary were sighted in 1879. The airport has scheduled services from Britain, as well as international charter flights, and serves the west and northwest.

Belfast is served by two airports. Belfast International at Aldergrove, the principal gateway, is 30km from the city centre, but the motorway link is excellent. British Airways and British Midland both run shuttle services between Aldergrove and London Heathrow and have connections with other major British cities. Travellers from North America on scheduled flights are usually routed through London or Shannon, but American Trans Air flies directly from the US to Belfast.

Belfast City Airport, only 7km from the city centre, receives flights from London Gatwick and Luton Airport (about 30km from London), and from other UK provincial airports. (See **Arriving** pages 178–9.)

By sea

Cruise liners, such as the *QEII*, call at Cobh, Co Cork. However, travel by sea nowadays tends to be a crossing by car ferry from Britain or France.

All major routes to the Republic, apart from Liverpool to Dublin, start in Wales: Holyhead for Dublin and Dun Laoghaire; Fishguard for Rosslare; Pembroke for Rosslare; and Swansea for Cork.

Northern Ireland is served from the Scottish ports of Cairnryan (to Larne), Stranraer (to Belfast), Campbeltown (to Ballycastle) and from Liverpool (to Belfast). There are also services to Rosslare from Cherbourg and Roscoff, and also to Cork from Roscoff. (See **Arriving** page 179.)

GETTING AROUND

Ireland is a small country (though probably much larger than most visitors expect) and communications are generally good.

By bus

Long distance services are operated by Irish Bus (Bus Éireann) in the Republic and Ulsterbus in Northern Ireland. Both offer a reasonably efficient and inexpensive method of travel, especially in areas infrequently serviced (or in some cases not served at all) by rail. City bus services, particularly in Dublin and Belfast, are excellent.

It is possible to travel between Britain and Ireland by bus – although not the quickest way, it is certainly economical. Services are operated by Eurolines, based in Britain (tel: 0990–143219 if calling from within Britain).

By car

This is the best way of getting around Ireland. Roads are generally good – and getting better – on both sides of the border. The old image of the Irish road as a pot-holed ribbon of mud has long since given way to modern experience as many improvement schemes, often funded by the European Union, speed ahead.

By rail

Rail services in the Republic are operated by the state-owned Irish Rail (Iarnród Éireann). Trains are comfortable and generally reliable and the fares reasonable. There are two classes of travel: standard (2nd class) and super standard (1st class). Major towns and ports are easily reached from Dublin, but there are large gaps in the system, especially in the northwest.

Northern Ireland Railways, also state-owned, operates between Belfast and Londonderry, Larne, Bangor and Dublin. The Belfast-Dublin Express travels non-stop between the two cities in two hours. There are eight trains a day in each direction, with five on Sundays.

Further details on rail services are contained in the *Thomas Cook European Timetable*, published monthly. (See **Public Transport** page 187.)

THE REGIONS

Ireland's ancient provinces – Ulster, Munster, Leinster and Connacht – roughly divide the country into north, south, east and west.

Ulster is an unbelievably beautiful region. North of Belfast, the Antrim Coast Road, leading to the Giant's Causeway, is unquestionably one of the world's most beautiful coastal routes, presenting a kaleidoscope of picturesque glens, villages and fishing harbours. For mountain-lovers there are the Mountains of Mourne, sweeping down to the sea in Co Down, and the Sperrins in Co Tyrone. The Fermanagh Lakelands are a Valhalla for boaters and anglers.

Munster extends southwards from Galway Bay to Mizen Head and the island of Cape Clear, and eastwards to Waterford. Soaring cliffs punctuate a coastline of rocky coves and soft, sandy beaches. Here are the ancient places: Viking Limerick and Waterford; the forts of Dingle Peninsula; and the legendary Rock of Cashel.

Leinster stretches from the border of Ulster south to Co Wexford, and from the Irish Sea to the River Shannon. Here the clan rulers built the great burial mound at Newgrange, and later the High Kings of Ireland ruled from the Hill of Tara. Brian Ború defeated the Vikings at Clontarf, near Dublin, in 1014, and in 1690 William of Orange's victory at the Battle of the Boyne set up a chain of events that continues to the present day.

Connacht, the far west of Ireland, is a land of wide horizons with mountains brooding over the ever-changing Atlantic Ocean on one side and the fertile plains of the Shannon Valley on the other. To the south, medieval Galway City gazes out towards the Aran Isles, and in the north Benbulben dominates Sligo and the landscapes that inspired W B Yeats.

Jaunting car, ideal for getting about

THE BORDER

The border between the Republic and Northern Ireland, created in 1921 by Britain's Government of Ireland Act, loops from the western shore of Lough Foyle to Carlingford Lough, just south of Newry, Co Down.

Under the Act, six of Ulster's nine counties – Antrim, Armagh, Down, Fermanagh, Londonderry and Tyrone – were retained as part of the United Kingdom. Cavan, Donegal and Monaghan, part of the Republic, are the remaining counties.

The border left a number of communities effectively straddling two jurisdictions – no problem during peaceful times (apart from creating opportunities for smuggling), but a security hazard when violence arose.

Now the border stands as a symbol of a divided Ireland, and it underscores the ambivalence implied in the North by the question, 'Are you British or are you Irish?'. The people of Northern Ireland can choose between an Irish or British passport – many pragmatists carry both. The removal of customs and immigration barriers in the European Union has effectively removed frontiers between member-states, but has made little difference to the mental divide between north and south in Ireland.

In terms of everyday travel, however, the border has never been a truly formidable frontier. Even at the height of the Troubles, when British Army patrols were much in evidence and drivers had to zig-zag through barbed-wire barriers, the business of passing from one country to another was completed with little of the formality and tension found in other parts of the world.

Statue of William of Orange, who landed at Carrickfergus in 1690

The casual nature of the border is underscored by the Shannon-Erne Waterway, which traverses counties Leitrim, Cavan and Fermanagh to link the rivers Shannon and Erne. Opened in 1993, the restored waterway flits back and forth across the border – and is itself the border in some places – but nowhere along its 63km length is there a checkpoint or Customs post; instead the waterway is occupied only by boats and pleasure cruisers.

LIFESTYLE AND ETIQUETTE

A modern phrase sums up perfectly a lifestyle which has prevailed in Ireland since the first Celtic herdsman reclined on the turf with a happy sigh. The phrase is 'laid back'.

Time, they will tell you in Ireland, is the one asset each of us has in equal measure: 24 hours of it replenished every single day. Most of us treat it like money – budgeting it, counting it, auditing it, and trying to make a profit from it. The Irish regard it as part of their heritage; an heirloom to be cherished like a work of art. Time is too precious to be squandered on mundane commerce.

A conversation struck up with a fellow passenger on a

Time to stand and watch the world

bus can have either or both of you missing the stop.

A visit to the pub can extend well beyond the limit you set yourself, for there is no such thing in Ireland as a quick drink. Warmly, easily, you are drawn into the conversation, questioned but not cross-examined, listened to with

Dublin's Abbey Theatre is famous for plays by Irish writers about the Irish

courtesy and humour.

Old-fashioned courtesy and hospitality thrive in Ireland. Men still hold doors open for women and give up their seats for them on buses and trains – though the obverse of that coin is an equally old-fashioned chauvinism.

The basic rule for visitors is: 'Be garrulous.' When you are addressed do reply, and fully. Better still, get in first with a greeting and a comment on the weather. But never initiate discussion on issues the Irish are particularly sensitive about – especially abortion, divorce, religion and The North.

WHAT TO SEE

'There lay the green shore
of Ireland, like some coast of plenty.
We could see towns, towers,
churches, harvests; but the curse of
800 years we could not discern.'

R W EMERSON,
English Traits, 1856

Leinster

*L*einster is a province of varied and lovely scenery, with fascinating bogland, fish-filled lakes, the River Shannon, nature reserves, sandy beaches, stately homes and castles. There are more counties here than the other three provinces – 12 of the 32 – plus the Republic's capital, Dublin.

DUBLIN CITY
ABBEY THEATRE
Founded in 1904 by W B Yeats and friends for the performance of plays by, and about, the Irish – Yeats, Synge, Shaw, O'Casey and others have had plays premièred here (see page 58). It incorporates the smaller Peacock Theatre.
Lower Abbey Street, Dublin 1.
Tel: 01–878 7222.

BANK OF IRELAND
This magnificent 18th-century building, with its huge multi-coloured porticoes and sculptured figures, was originally designed as the Irish Parliament House. When Parliament ceased to exist after the Act of Union in 1800, the Bank of Ireland bought the building. The former House of Lords can be seen on a tour. The old bank armoury houses the Story of Banking Museum.
2 College Green, Dublin 2. Tel: 01–677 6801. Open: Monday to Friday 10am–4pm (to 5pm Thursday); tours: 10.30am, 11.30am and 1.45pm. Free. Museum: Tuesday to Friday 10am–4pm. Admission charge.

CHESTER BEATTY LIBRARY AND GALLERY OF ORIENTAL ART
Donated to the country by Sir Alfred Chester Beatty (1875–1968), exhibits include manuscripts ranging from biblical papyri to Persian Korans, prints, wall hangings and Oriental artefacts.
Relocating to Dublin Castle late 1999.

The exquisite Chinese ceiling in the Chester Beatty Library and Gallery of Oriental Art

CHRIST CHURCH CATHEDRAL
The Church of Ireland (Anglican) cathedral is Dublin's oldest building, and was founded in 1038 by Sitric Silkenbeard, King of the Dublin Norsemen, who built a simple wooden church here. It was later rebuilt in stone by Richard de Clare, Earl of Pembroke (known as Strongbow) in 1169. There is a monument to Strongbow in the nave. The 12th-century crypt contains interesting relics including 17th-century punishment stocks which once stood in the churchyard.

CITY HALL

The seat of Dublin Corporation since 1852, City Hall was built between 1769 and 1779 as the Royal Exchange. It was the scene of the Irish Volunteer rallies in the 1780s, and Government troops used it as a barracks and torture chamber during the 1798 rebellion. It has a beautiful domed entrance hall.

Lord Edward Street, Dublin 2. Tel: 01–679 6111. Open: Monday to Friday 9am–1pm, 2.15–5pm. Free.

LEINSTER

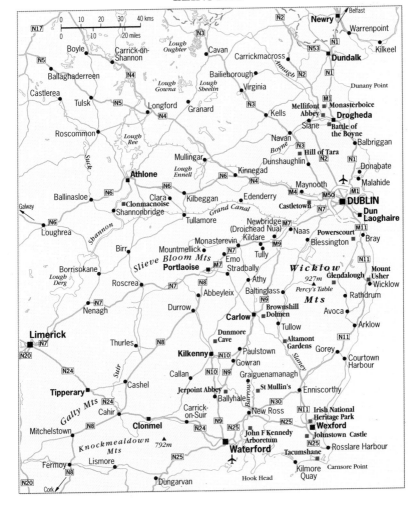

CUSTOM HOUSE

This 18th-century building, designed by James Gandon, was severely damaged by fire in 1921. Extensive restoration work was finally completed in 1991. A visitor centre features a Gandon museum.
Custom House Quay, Dublin 1. Tel: 01–878 7660. Open: Monday to Friday 10am–5pm, weekends 2–5pm. Closed Monday and Tuesday, November to mid-March. Admission charge.

DUBLIN CASTLE

Built in the early 13th century, only one of the four Norman towers – the Record Tower – survives. Presidents of Ireland have been inaugurated in lofty St Patrick's Hall since 1938, and foreign dignitaries are hosted in the elegant State Apartments (see page 57).
Dame Street, Dublin 2. Tel: 01–677 7129. Open: Monday to Friday 10am–5pm, weekends and public holidays 2–5pm. Times may vary because of state functions. Admission charge.

DUBLIN CIVIC MUSEUM

Devoted to the history of local commerce, industry, transport and politics, exhibits include coins from the Dublin Vikings' mint, flint axes, old maps and views of Dublin. Exhibitions on Dublin life are held periodically.

58 South William Street, Dublin 2. Tel: 01–679 4260. Open: Tuesday to Saturday 10am–6pm, Sunday 11am–2pm. Free.

DUBLIN EXPERIENCE

This multi-media interpretation of Dublin and its people from the 10th century to modern times is a useful and entertaining 45-minute presentation, best seen before sightseeing.
Thomas Davis Theatre, Trinity College Campus, Dublin 2. Tel: 01–608 1688. Open: late May to September, daily 10am–5pm. Admission charge.

DUBLIN WRITERS' MUSEUM

Opened in 1991, the museum has paintings and busts of many of Dublin's major writers, as well as memorabilia and rare books. There is a lecture theatre, temporary exhibitions, a children's book section and a centre where Irish authors can meet, carry out research and work.
18 Parnell Square, Dublin 1. Tel: 01–872 2077. Open: Monday to Saturday

Sumptuous furnishings for the State Drawing Rooms in Dublin Castle

10am–5pm (to 6pm, Monday to Friday, June to August), Sunday and public holidays 11am–6pm. Admission charge.

DUBLIN ZOO
Open for over 160 years, this is one of the few zoos where lions have bred in captivity, one achieving worldwide fame as the MGM film lion. There is a large collection of wild animals and birds, some endangered, from many countries, as well as information panels, a pets' corner and a train ride around the zoo.
Phoenix Park, Dublin 8. Tel: 01–677 1425. Open: daily 9.30am–6pm (from 10.30am Sunday). Admission charge.

FOUR COURTS
Architect James Gandon produced a masterpiece with this building, opened in 1802, which houses the law courts of Chancery, King's Bench, Exchequer and Common Pleas. It was badly damaged in 1922, at the outbreak of civil war; a three-day battle ended with an explosion destroying many of Ireland's historical records and official deeds (see page 59).
Inns Quay, Dublin 8. Tel: 01–872 5555. Open: weekdays 11am–1pm, 2–4pm. Free.

GENERAL POST OFFICE
The imposing GPO building, with its Ionic portico and fluted pillars, was completed in 1818 and virtually destroyed in the Easter Rising of 1916 (see page 59). It reopened in 1929. Inside is a bronze statue of the dying Cuchulainn, leader of the Red Branch Knights in Irish mythology.
O'Connell Street, Dublin 1. Tel: 01–872 8888. Open: Monday to Saturday 8am–8pm, Sunday and public holidays 10.30am–6.30pm.

GUINNESS HOP STORE
A cooperage display and transport gallery relating to the Guinness Empire are housed in a four-storey, 19th-century hop store on the brewery's original 26-hectare site. The World of Guinness Exhibition includes an audio-visual presentation showing the history and manufacture of Dublin's most famous product. Guinness can be sampled at the Hop Store bar.
St James's Gate, Dublin 8. Tel: 01–408 4800. Open: Monday to Saturday 9.30am–4pm (to 5pm, April to September), Sunday and public holidays noon–4pm (10.30am–4pm, April to September). Admission charge.

The 'Cooper' demonstrates his skills at the World of Guinness Exhibition

TOWN LIFE

A town, the dictionaries say, is a place with a large number of dwellings; a densely populated settlement with a concentration of commerce. The word implies an increased pace, sophistication and a degree of stress.

In Ireland, still largely rural in spite of shopping malls, leisure centres and EU-funded highways, a town is often best described as a coming together of pubs around a square in which one may trade on market days and gossip the whole year round.

Many of the larger towns are still small enough for the surrounding countryside – the fields, forests and mountains – to be visible from their centres. Even in metropolitan Dublin the eye can move in a single sweep from a group of dinner-jacketed, ball-gowned students crossing Grafton Street after an all-night party to a man decorously clad in tweed suit and green wellington boots.

The closeness of the land to Irish town life is underscored by the greengrocers' stores, often quite small places with rough-and-ready displays of fruit and vegetables – slightly battered-looking apples, carrots with the earth still clinging – and an absence of plastic pre-packaging. Everything looks as if it has been harvested just down the road, as indeed it probably has.

There is a delightfully old-fashioned ambience: crowded hardware store windows filled with unidentifiable – often indescribable – bits and pieces of

Street life and street character

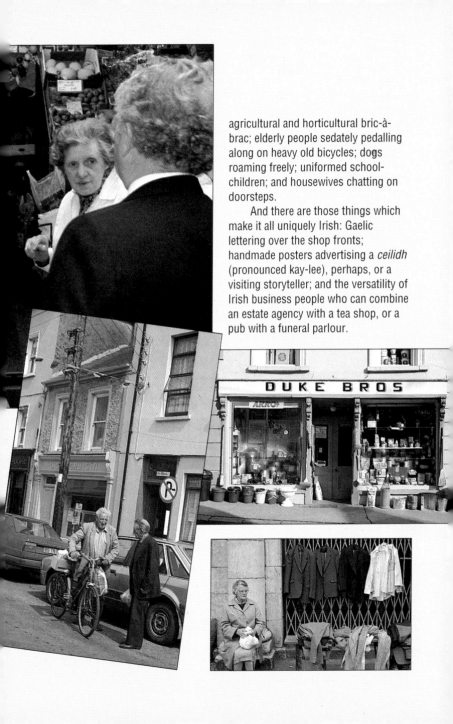

agricultural and horticultural bric-à-brac; elderly people sedately pedalling along on heavy old bicycles; dogs roaming freely; uniformed school-children; and housewives chatting on doorsteps.

And there are those things which make it all uniquely Irish: Gaelic lettering over the shop fronts; handmade posters advertising a *ceilidh* (pronounced kay-lee), perhaps, or a visiting storyteller; and the versatility of Irish business people who can combine an estate agency with a tea shop, or a pub with a funeral parlour.

JAMES JOYCE CENTRE

The literary display in this impressive Georgian house includes biographies of characters from *Ulysses* based on Dublin people whom Joyce knew. Walking tours of the author's Dublin are organised.
35 North Great George's Street, Dublin 1. Tel: 01–878 8547. Open: Monday to Saturday 9.30am–5pm, Sunday 12.30–5pm. Admission charge.

KILMAINHAM GAOL

History covering an eventful century and a half is almost tangible at Kilmainham Gaol, erected in 1796. Now a museum pinpointing Irish political and penal history from the 1780s to the 1920s, the old gaol still presents a gruesome atmosphere.

Eamonn de Valera, former leader of Fianna Fáil, Taoiseach (Prime Minister), and later President, was one of the last prisoners to be held here. Years later, in 1966, he officially declared open the Kilmainham Gaol Museum.

Exhibits at Kilmainham Gaol evoke the bleak reality of a term of imprisonment

A fascinating audio-visual presentation gives a 30-minute outline of Irish nationalism over a 200-year period.
Kilmainham, Dublin 8. Tel: 01–453 5984. Open: April to September, daily 9.30am–4.45pm; October to March, Monday to Friday 9.30am–4pm, Sunday 10am–4.45pm. Admission charge.

LEINSTER HOUSE

The Dáil (lower house) and Seanad (senate) of the Irish Parliament convene in this lavish building, which was constructed in 1745 as the town house of the Dukes of Leinster. Tours of the government buildings take place each Saturday.
Kildare Street, Dublin 2. Tours: Saturday 10.30am–3.30pm. Ticket office: National Gallery (see page 32). Free.

THE LIBERTIES

This area in the southwest of the city covers around 80 hectares. Historically, the name originates from privileges bestowed under Magna Carta. Today it is an interesting precinct of markets, bargain shops, betting shops, churches and pubs.

> ### KILMAINHAM'S INMATES
> Eamonn de Valera, born in New York of Irish ancestry, strongly influenced Irish politics over a long period. His spell in gaol was for his part in the 1916 Easter Rising; he was released in 1924. One of de Valera's predecessors in Kilmainham was Home Rule Party leader Charles Stewart Parnell. Leaders of the Easter Rising were executed at the gaol, among them Con Colbert, Padraig Pearse and James Connolly.

MARSH'S LIBRARY

Dating from 1701, this is Ireland's oldest public library. Inside are 'cages' in which readers were locked to prevent theft. *St Patrick's Close, Dublin 8. Tel: 01–454 3511. Open: Monday, Wednesday to Friday 10am–12.45pm, 2–5pm, Saturday 10.30am–12.45pm. Donation appreciated.*

NATIONAL BOTANIC GARDENS

Twenty thousand different plant species are set in 19.5 hectares of rock, herb and rose gardens and herbaceous borders, and in the superb mid-19th-century glasshouses, designed and built by Richard Turner. The gardens, beside the River Tolka, date from 1795.

DUBLIN

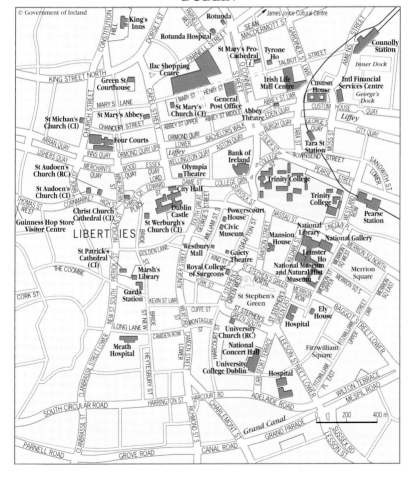

*Glasnevin, Dublin 9. Tel: 01–837 4388.
Open: Monday to Saturday 9am–6pm,
Sunday 11am–6pm (winter, Monday to
Saturday 10am–4.30pm, Sunday
11am–4.30pm (greenhouses open for fewer
hours). Free.*

NATIONAL GALLERY OF IRELAND

The gallery houses Ireland's foremost
collection of paintings, including works
by Rembrandt, Reynolds, El Greco and
Goya. Every major European school of
painting is represented among its
thousands of exhibits. Vestments, objets
d'art and 300 pieces of sculpture are
also exhibited. Irish painters are strongly
represented, with works by George
Barrett, Francis Danby and James

Latham, among others.
*Merrion Square West, Dublin 2. Tel:
01–661 5133. Open: Monday to Saturday
10am–5.30pm (to 8.30pm Thursday),
Sunday 2–5pm. Tours: Saturday 3pm,
Sunday 2.15, 3 and 4pm. Free.*

NATIONAL LIBRARY

This treasure-house of information
about Ireland has many books, including
first editions, complete files of Irish
magazines and newspapers, maps,
prints, drawings and photographs.
Tickets issued for reading the books.
*Kildare Street, Dublin 2. Tel: 01–661 8811.
Open: Monday 10am–9pm, Tuesday and
Wednesday 2–9pm, Thursday and Friday
10am–5pm, Saturday 10am–1pm. Free.*

NATIONAL MUSEUM OF IRELAND, COLLINS BARRACKS

Collins Barracks, the oldest military
barracks in Europe, acquired by the
National Museum in 1994, is the site of
a new museum of the decorative arts
and of economic, social, political and
military history of Ireland. Items on
display include a life belt and oar
salvaged from the *Lusitania*.
*Collins Barracks, Benburb Street, Dublin 7.
Tel: 01–677 7444. Open: Tuesday to
Saturday 10am–5pm, Sunday 2–5pm. Free.*

NATIONAL MUSEUM OF IRELAND, KILDARE STREET

Opened in 1890, the museum was the
result of merging several collections. It
comprises the Irish Antiquities, Art and
Natural History divisions, and contains
artefacts and masterpieces dating
from the first century AD to the 16th
century. Among notable exhibits are the

The National Gallery of Ireland is a treasure
house of European and Irish artwork

8th-century Ardagh Chalice, and the 12th-century Cross of Cong. The music room has a display of Irish harps.
Kildare Street, Dublin 2. Tel: 01–677 7444. Open: Tuesday to Saturday 10am–5pm, Sunday 2–5pm. Free.

NATIONAL WAX MUSEUM

Among life-size Irish historical, political and literary figures in wax are Irish and international stars from the worlds of sport and entertainment. Exhibitions include Children's World of Fairytale and Fantasy, the Hall of Megastars, a replica of da Vinci's *Last Supper*, and a Chamber of Horrors (see page 59).
Granby Row, Parnell Square, Dublin 1. Tel: 01–872 6340. Open: Monday to Saturday 10am–5.30pm, Sunday noon–5.30pm. Admission charge.

NATURAL HISTORY MUSEUM

This zoological museum has a large collection of the vertebrate and invertebrate wildlife of Ireland. As well as mammals, birds, butterflies and other insects, fish, fowl and mammals from Africa and Asia are displayed, including skeletons of prehistoric animals.
Merrion Street, Dublin 2. Tel: 01–677 7444. Open: Tuesday to Saturday 10am–5pm, Sunday 2–5pm. Free.

OLD JAMESON DISTILLERY

The Jameson Distillery was converted into the head offices of Irish Distillers after it closed in 1972. The old distillery can be visited on a guided tour. There are working models of the distilling process, an audio-visual presentation on Irish whiskey, and a sampling of the goods in the Jameson bar afterwards.
Bow Street, Smithfield, Dublin 7. Tel: 01–807 2355. Open: daily 9.30am–6pm (last tour 5pm). Admission charge.

Delightful walk along the River Tolka at the National Botanic Gardens

PHOENIX PARK

One of the largest enclosed public parks in the world with 710 hectares, Phoenix Park was laid out in the 18th century. Its name *(fionn uisce)* means 'clear water'. It contains lakes, gardens, woods, a herd of deer and a zoo (see page 27), with space for soccer, Gaelic football, hurling, cricket and polo. The residences of the Irish President and the US Ambassador, and the headquarters of the Garda (police), with a small police museum and a visitor centre, are also in the park.
West of Heuston Station, Dublin 8. Open: daily. Police museum – tel: 01–677 1156. Open: Monday to Friday 9am–5pm. Free.

Visitor centre – tel: 01–677 0095. Open: all year weekends; mid-March to October, daily 10am–5pm.

POWERSCOURT TOWN HOUSE CENTRE

Converted in the 1980s into a highly sophisticated, traffic-free precinct of select shops, cafés, craft shops and boutiques, these former wholesale textile company's premises were originally built between 1771 and 1774 as the town mansion of the Powerscourt family. *South William Street, Dublin 2. Tel: 01–679 4144. Open: Monday to Saturday 9am–6pm, except public holidays.*

ROYAL CANAL

A pleasant waterway with more than 11km of towpath winding through northern Dublin, the Royal Canal never reached its full potential as a cargo-carrying connection between the Liffey and the Shannon; the Grand Canal, passing through the city's southern suburbs, was already fulfilling that role. Long John Binns, a shoemaker, founded The Royal as a rival waterway in 1789. It lost money from the start, though the canal endures to this day as a leisure attraction. Some still call it the Shoemaker's Canal.

ROYAL HOSPITAL

Kilmainham's Royal Hospital is Ireland's only surviving fully classical 17th-century building. It was designed by William Robinson in the 1680s to house retired and disabled soldiers. It officially passed to the Irish Free State in 1922, and subsequently became the headquarters of the Garda (Irish police). Extensive restorations were carried out in 1980. The government designated the building the National Centre for Culture and the Arts and its interior is considered among the finest in Dublin. It houses the **Irish Museum of Modern Art**, whose excellent displays of international art include works by Picasso, and Irish art of the 20th century. In the grounds are two cemeteries: one is believed to contain the body of Irish patriot Robert Emmet who led the 1803 rising and was executed. British soldiers who died in the 1916 Rising occupy the other, along with army pensioners. *Military Road, Dublin 8. Tel: 01–671 8666 (museum: 01–612 9900). Hospital – open: July and August, Tuesday to Sunday noon–5pm; rest of year, Tuesday to Saturday 2–5pm. Free, but a charge may be made for special events. Museum – open: Tuesday to Saturday 10am–5.30pm, Sunday noon–5.30pm. Free.*

For over 240 years – until 1927 – generations of old soldiers were residents at the Royal Hospital, Kilmainham

James Joyce

*J*ames Joyce, one of Ireland's greatest writers, spent most of his life outside the country, but he wrote only about Dublin and Dubliners. He knew the city so well and used its detail so minutely in his works, that it was claimed if Dublin were to be totally destroyed, his novel *Ulysses* could be used as a blueprint to rebuild it.

Born in 1882 at 41 Brighton Square, in Rathgar, 5km from the city centre, Joyce lived at more than 20 other addresses before leaving Dublin at the age of 22. After that he wrote about the city as he travelled abroad.

Between 1893 and 1898 he attended Belvedere College in Great Denmark Street before studying at University College Dublin. At 35 North Great George's Street is the James Joyce Centre (see page 30) whose library and archives attract serious students of the writer and his work.

Each year, 16 June – the day on which the whole action of *Ulysses* takes place – sees special Bloomsday events throughout the city and at the Ormond Hotel on Upper Ormond Quay, a meeting place for Leopold Bloom, the principal character in the book.

Bronze statue of Joyce in honour of his famous novel *Ulysses*

A short walk from the eastern end of Railway Street is the DART system's Connolly Station, from where Joyce fans can take a train two stops to Pearse Station, south of the Liffey. Just outside the station is Westland Row, at the end of which is Sweny's pharmacy, remaining much as it is described in *Ulysses*.

Sandymount Strand, a 5km beach between Ringsend and Booterstown, is another *Ulysses* setting and was a favourite spot with Joyce and his wife, Nora Barnacle. The Martello tower at Sandycove, featured in the first chapter of *Ulysses*, is now the James Joyce Museum (see page 44).

LITERARY IRELAND

No other small country has produced as many big names in the world of literature as Ireland – names that confront the visitor in each of the ancient provinces.

Dublin has so many associations with literature that in 1991 it opened a Writers' Museum at 18 Parnell Square North (see page 26).

Lovers of James Joyce can follow the steps of his *Ulysses* character, Leopold Bloom, through the streets of Dublin and visit the Martello tower at Sandycove (see page 44), where the author lived for a short time. As a young man, the dramatist George Bernard Shaw lived briefly with his family at Torca Cottage, up nearby Dalkey Hill.

Jonathan Swift, author of *Gulliver's Travels*, is buried in Dublin's St Patrick's Cathedral, where he served as Dean from 1713 to 1745. Swift attended Kilkenny College, where playwrights William Congreve and George Farquhar also studied.

Edith Somerville and Violet Martin Ross, the authors of the hilarious *Experiences of an Irish RM*, lived in Castletownshend, near Skibbereen, Co Cork. They are buried in the cemetery of St Barrahane's Church.

The Yeats Trail through Sligo and Leitrim is a 160km signposted tour through locations immortalised by the poet W B Yeats and his artist brother Jack.

Ulster also has its share of great names. Oscar Wilde and Samuel Beckett were pupils at Portora Royal School, Enniskillen. Louis MacNeice grew up at Carrickfergus overlooking Belfast Lough and C S Lewis was

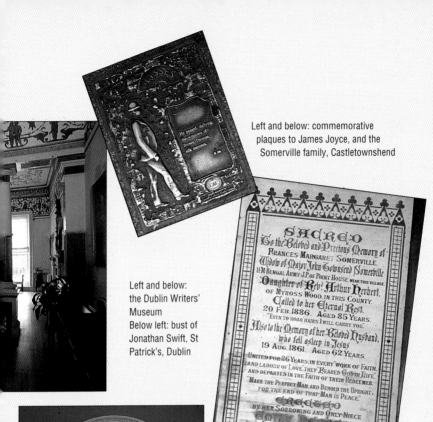

Left and below: commemorative plaques to James Joyce, and the Somerville family, Castletownshend

Left and below: the Dublin Writers' Museum
Below left: bust of Jonathan Swift, St Patrick's, Dublin

a Belfast man. But the province is best known now for its contemporary writers – such names as Benedict Kelly, John Montague and Seamus Heaney.

Irish Literature dates from about AD600. It was exposed to European influences by writers such as Pádraic Pearse (1879–1916) and Pádraic Ó Conaire (1883–1928). Among other distinguished writers in Irish were Liam O Flaitheartaigh (O'Flaherty) and Brendan Behan.

ST ANNE'S PARK ROSE GARDEN

A mecca for the rose specialist in the centre of Dublin Corporation's public park, the gardens were created in conjunction with Clontarf Horticultural Society. More than 100 numbered and catalogued varieties of floribunda, hybrid tea, old shrub roses and miniatures bloom in summer.

Clontarf, Dublin 3 (off the Howth road). Guided tours available by arrangement with the Parks Department (tel: 01–833 1941), or Clontarf Horticultural Society (tel: 01–872 1076). Open at all times.

ST AUDOEN'S CHURCH OF IRELAND (Anglican)

One of the oldest churches in Dublin, near a preserved stretch of the city wall and minus much of its roof, St Audoen's is dated variously from AD650 to 1169. A pre-Norse church of St Columcille once stood on the site. The tower contains three bells cast in 1423, said to be the oldest in Ireland. In the porch is an early Christian gravestone, known as the 'Lucky Stone', which has been kept at the church since before 1309 (see page 57).

High Street, Dublin 8.

Detailed wood carving on St Michan's organ, which dates from around 1725

ST AUDOEN'S ROMAN CATHOLIC CHURCH

Next door to St Audoen's Church of Ireland, is the Roman Catholic church, dating from the 1840s. 'The Flame on the Hill', an audio-visual presentation telling the story of the history of Christianity in Ireland, is shown at the church.

High Street, Dublin 8. Open: daily 10am–4.30pm. Admission charge.

ST MICHAN'S CHURCH

The original 1095 Danish church was almost completely rebuilt in the 1680s and restored in the 19th century. The finely carved 18th-century organ in the Anglican church is believed to have been played by Handel while composing *The Messiah* in the year which saw its first public performance at Neale's New Music Hall in Fishamble Street. Probably the main 'attraction' at St Michan's is a tour of the vaults, where a number of corpses, some from the 17th century, can be viewed in an extraordinarily well-preserved state (see page 59).

Lower Church Street, Dublin 8. Tel: 01–872 4154. Open: Monday to Friday 10am–12.45pm, 2–4.45pm, Saturday 10am–12.45pm. Donation appreciated.

ST PATRICK'S CATHEDRAL

St Patrick is said to have baptised converts to the Christian faith in a well which once existed adjacent to the present National Cathedral of the Church of Ireland. Because of the sacred association with St Patrick, a church has stood here since the 5th century. A Norman church was built on the site in 1191, and re-building took place in the first half of the 13th century, resulting in the magnificent edifice which exists today. Jonathan Swift, Dean of St Patrick's for more than 30 years, is buried in the nave, and there is a marble bust of him in the south aisle (see page 57).

Patrick's Close, Dublin 8. Tel: 01–475 4817. Open: Monday to Friday 9am–6pm, Saturday 9am–5pm (4pm in winter), Sunday 9.30–11am, 12.45–3pm, 4.15–5pm (April to September), 10–11am, 12.45–3pm (October to March). Admission charge.

Above: St Patrick's Cathedral was extensively restored in the 1860s

Left: paper marbling – one of a wide range of crafts at Tower Design

TOWER DESIGN GUILD

Heraldic artistry, silk painting, wood carving, pewter engineering, etching, pottery and designer knitting are among the crafts which can be seen here. A shop sells a range of craft products.

IDA Enterprise Centre, Pearse Street, Dublin 2. Tel: 01–677 5655. Open: Monday to Friday 9am–5.30pm, some units closed 1–2pm. Shop: Monday to Friday 10am–5pm. Free.

WATERWAYS VISITOR CENTRE

This informative centre uses audio-visual facilities and exhibitions to interpret the historical role of Ireland's navigable waterways over the years, and their development into a valuable public amenity.

Grand Canal Basin, Ringsend, Dublin 2. Tel: 01–661 3111. Open: June to September, daily 9.30am–6pm; October to May, Wednesday to Sunday, 12.30–5pm. Admission charge.

Trinity College

*O*ne of Dublin's three universities, Trinity is situated in busy College Green in the heart of the city. It was built on the site of an Augustinian Priory, All Hallows. Through the great arched gate, with its statues of two famous graduates, Oliver Goldsmith and Edmund Burke, is a spacious area of lawns and cobbled squares, and gardens surrounded by buildings of various architectural styles and periods. The oldest part of the college is the Rubrics, a row of red-brick buildings dating from 1700.

Queen Elizabeth I founded Trinity College, the sole college of Dublin University, in 1592 as a seat of learning and the establishment of 'true religion' within the realm. Protestantism was the Queen's religion, and for centuries Catholics were prohibited from Trinity.

Today, Trinity College caters for around 8,000 students, following in the footsteps of such illustrious literary giants as Jonathan Swift, Samuel Beckett, Oscar Wilde and Bram Stoker. Women students have been admitted since 1903.

The tall campanile near the centre of Library Square was erected in 1853. Beyond it, screened by gracious maple trees and old lamps, is the famous library which houses many ancient volumes in the Long Room, including the famous *Book of Kells*.

Sculpture outside Trinity's Library

St Patrick's Day Parade, 17 March, is celebrated in style in Dublin

The Long Room itself warrants inspection, with its barrel-vaulted ceiling 12.2m high, and tall shelves of leather-bound books, many of them accessible only by narrow ladder (but not by the public). Altogether, Trinity has more than two and a half million books.

To the right of the entrance to the college is the Examination Hall, a former theatre. Its massive blackened doors must have struck terror in the heart of many a candidate. The hall is sometimes used for concerts. Like the Chapel opposite, which is shared by all Christian denominations, it

THE *BOOK OF KELLS*

The *Book of Kells* is a richly coloured, minutely detailed version of the Gospels, written in Latin on vellum. Originally one volume, the vast book, regarded as one of the world's finest illuminated manuscripts, was divided into four when repairs were carried out in the 1950s. Two of these, opened at intricately decorated pages, can be closely examined by visitors (but be prepared for crowds). The '*Book of Kells* Turning Darkness into Light' is a major exhibition which opened in early 1999.

ST PATRICK

St Patrick's Day, 17 March, is marked in Ireland, the United States and other parts of the world with parades and cheering crowds. But the carnival spirit is a fairly recent development, evolved mainly in North America. Once, St Patrick's Day in Ireland was a very sombre affair, with the pubs closed and parades of industrial floats – more in line with the hair-shirt zeal of the saint and his contemporaries.

Born in the west of Roman Britain about AD389, Patrick led a restless life. As a boy he was captured by Irish pirates and taken to Co Antrim, where he was sold into slavery. After six years he escaped, trained as a missionary and returned to Ireland 37 years later. He dedicated the rest of his life – some sources say he reached the age of 104 – to challenging the druids and converting the kings of Ireland to Christianity. Until the late 17th century the Irish never used Patrick as a first name out of respect. Now one in four males is named after him.

has a barrel-vaulted ceiling and notable plasterwork. Near the Chapel is the college Dining Hall, which sometimes doubles as an examination room. The Arts Building houses the multi-media Dublin Experience (see page 26).

Trinity was used for the campus scenes in the 1983 film, *Educating Rita*. *College Green, Dublin 2. Tel: 01–608 2320. Grounds – open: daily 8am–10pm. Freely accessible. Library – open: Monday to Saturday 9.30am–5pm, Sunday noon–4.30pm (from 9.30am June to September). Admission charge.*

Fine plants and wide views at Fernhill Gardens, renowned for their camellias and rhododendrons

CO DUBLIN
BEECH PARK
Beech Park's unique collection of herbaceous and alpine plants, some very rare, is set in the old walled garden of a Regency house, and includes woodland plants, New Zealand daisies and a Georgian hothouse used for propagation. *Clonsilla. Tel: 01–821 2216. Open: March to October, first weekend of every month 2–6pm; July and August, Sunday and public holidays. Admission charge.*

CASINO
Just north of Dublin, this 18th-century former summerhouse – not a casino in the gambling sense – is in the Palladian style. Pillars, stone lions and balustrades provide generous ornamentation, while inside there are elaborate plaster ceilings. Built for the 1st Earl of Charlemont, the Casino was restored in the early 1980s. *Malahide Road, Marino. Tel: 01–833 1618. Open: November and February to April, Wednesday and Sunday noon–4pm;*

May to October, daily 10am–5pm (later in summer). Admission charge.

DRIMNAGH CASTLE
Drimnagh is the only Irish castle retaining a flooded moat, complete with waterfowl. It has a restored great hall, a battlement tower with look-out posts, a coach house, a folly tower and gardens laid out in formal 17th-century style. *Longanile Road, Dublin 12. Tel: 01–450 2530. Open: mid–April to October, Wednesday, Saturday and Sunday 10am–5pm. Admission charge.*

FERNHILL GARDENS
These 100-hectare privately owned gardens are renowned for their camellias, rhododendrons, magnolias and azaleas. There is also a fine collection of trees more than 200 years old, a wild-flower meadow and a Victorian kitchen garden. *Sandyford. Tel: 01–295 6000. Open: March to November, Tuesday, Saturday, public holidays 11am–5pm, Sunday 2–6pm. Admission charge.*

FRY MODEL RAILWAY MUSEUM

Railway enthusiasts will enjoy this museum which has many scale models of Irish trains dating from 1832 to Dublin's modern DART system. Another feature is the intriguing layout which includes the River Liffey, the Hill of Howth and various other local landscapes.

Malahide Castle Demesne, Malahide. Tel: 01–846 3779. Open: April to September, Monday to Saturday 10am–1pm, 2–5pm (closed Friday in April, May and September), Sunday and public holiday 2–6pm; October to March, weekends and public holidays 2–5pm. Admission charge.

HOWTH CASTLE GARDENS

The gardens, adjoining the Deer park Hotel and Golf Courses, are best visited in May and early June. Started in 1854, they are famous for their rhododendrons – several thousands of them. Within the estate are the ruins of 16th-century Corr Castle and a neolithic dolmen known as Aideen's Grave. The oldest part of Howth Castle dates from 1464, but it has been altered in every century since. The castle is closed to the public, but admission to the gardens is free.

Howth Castle, Howth. Tel: 01–832 2624. Open: daily 8am–sunset. Free.

DUBLIN ENVIRONS

HOWTH - NATIONAL TRANSPORT MUSEUM

This small museum exhibits early fire engines, trucks, tractors and other vehicles. The Hill of Howth No 9 train and a Giant's Causeway tram are among the stars of the show.

Howth Castle Demesne, Howth. Tel: 01–832 0427. Open: June to August,

One of the many superbly restored exhibits at the National Transport Museum

(from 2pm Sunday); September to May Saturday, Sunday and public holidays 2–5pm. Admission charge.

MALAHIDE CASTLE

Except for a brief period when Cromwell evicted them, the Talbot family lived here continuously from 1185 to 1973, when the last Lord Talbot died. The Great Hall, which has a minstrels' gallery, contains many portraits, while the Oak Room and two drawing rooms contain 17th-, 18th- and 19th-century furniture. The castle has an antiques shop and there are picnic areas in the grounds.

Malahide. Tel: 01–846 2184. Open:

Monday to Saturday 10am–12.45pm, 2–5pm, Sunday and public holidays 11am–12.45pm, 2–6pm (reduced hours in winter). Admission charge.

NATIONAL MARITIME MUSEUM OF IRELAND

Housed in the 1837 Mariners' Church, this museum has, among many exhibits, an 11m French longboat captured in Bantry Bay in 1796, and a noted collection of model ships on display.

Haigh Terrace, Dun Laoghaire. Tel: 01–280 0969. Open: May to September, Tuesday to Sunday and public holidays 1–5pm. Admission charge.

JAMES JOYCE MUSEUM

The Martello tower where Joyce spent a few weeks in 1904 as a guest of Oliver St John Gogarty is featured in his novel *Ulysses*, with Gogarty as the character of Buck Mulligan. Built in 1804, the tower contains a selection of Joyce memorabilia – the piano and guitar he played, a cigar case, a cane, manuscripts and a death mask of the author cast on 13 January 1941.

Sandycove. Tel: 01– 280 9265/872 2077. Open: April to October, Monday to Saturday 10am–1pm, 2–5pm, Sunday and public holidays 2–6pm. By appointment in winter. Admission charge.

NEWBRIDGE HOUSE

This Georgian house, built in 1737 for the Cobbe family, is now owned by Dublin County Council. A wealth of paintings hangs in the drawing room, and cabinets display many antique curiosities brought back by the Cobbe family from their extensive world travels. The cobbled square has been restored and opened as a farm and museum of 18th-century rural life. There is also an

aviary and a doll museum.
*Donabate. Tel: 01–843 6534. Open: April
to September, Tuesday to Saturday
10am–1pm, 2–5pm, Sunday and public
holidays 2–6pm; October to March,
weekends and public holidays 2–5pm.
Admission charge.*

CO LOUTH
BATTLE OF THE BOYNE SITE
At the county borders of Louth and
Meath, a large orange and green sign
marks the site where the armies of
William of Orange and James II met in
battle in 1690. The places where each
side camped and where the river was
crossed are also marked. A trail leaflet is
available at the site.
7km west of Drogheda. Freely accessible.

MILLMOUNT MUSEUM
Contained in the buildings of an 18th-
century military barracks, are relics from
Drogheda's trade, manufacturing and
domestic past. One interesting exhibit is

a leather-covered circular coracle.
*Drogheda. Tel: 041–983 3097. Open:
Tuesday to Saturday 10am–6pm, Sunday
2.30–5.30pm. Admission charge.*

OLD MELLIFONT ABBEY
Little remains of Ireland's first
Cistercian monastery, founded in 1142,
though a substantial square gatehouse
still stands, along with the ruins of a
cloister, a two-storey octagonal lavabo
and a 13th-century chapter house.
*Tullyvallen, 10km west of Drogheda,
(signposted). Tel: 041–982 6459. Open:
May to mid-October, daily 10am–5pm (to
6.30pm in summer). Admission charge.*

PROLEEK DOLMEN
This 5,000-year-old massive mushroom-
like stone structure has a capstone
weighing over 46 tonnes. Near by is a
Bronze Age, wedge-shaped, gallery grave.
Ballymascanlon, north of Dundalk. Free.

Twelfth-century Malahide Castle

CO MEATH
BOYNE VALLEY
ARCHAEOLOGICAL SITE

The area known as Brú na Bóinne encompasses over 40 monuments, ranging from the massive megalithic tombs of Newgrange, Knowth and Dowth to a variety of standing stones and earthworks. Newgrange is one of Europe's most important Stone-Age sites. The Newgrange passage grave, over 4,000 years old and predating the Pyramids of Egypt, is an extraordinary sight. The mound over the tomb, constructed of water-rolled pebbles, rises to a height of 11m, and is surrounded by an incomplete circle of stones. The passage is lined with huge stones, and mysterious 'artwork' in the form of geometrical symbols and spirals can be seen inside. A roof box incorporated in the structure allows the rays of the rising sun to penetrate a narrow slit and engulf the chamber with light – just briefly, once a year at the winter solstice. This phenomenon is reproduced artificially for the benefit of visitors. The Brú na Bóinne Visitor Centre interprets the archaeological heritage of the area and is the starting point for visits by bus to Newgrange and Knowth. Dowth is currently closed to the public during excavations.

Visitor centre: Donore, 11km southwest of Drogheda. Tel: 041–982 4488. Open: March, April and October, daily 9.30am–5.30pm (to 5pm November to February); May to September, daily 9am–6.30pm (to 7pm June to August). Admission charge.

HILL OF TARA

Famous as the seat of the High Kings of Ireland and an important site since the Stone Age, when a passage tomb was built, this was a major political and religious centre in pre–Christian times. Commanding majestic views over the fertile plains of Meath, it was abandoned in AD1022 and now consists of grass-covered mounds, banks, wide ditches and earthworks. Inside the Mound of Hostages, a passage grave dated to 1,800 years BC, the skeleton of a boy wearing a necklace of bronze, amber and jet was found.

Tara, 13km south of Navan. Tel: 046–25903. Open: May to October, daily 10am–5pm (mid–June to mid–September, 9.30am–6.30pm). Guided tours available. Admission charge.

KELLS

Monks from Iona in Scotland took refuge in a monastery here after being evicted by the Danes. They devoted their time to writing the *Book of Kells*, which was removed to the safety of Trinity College, Dublin, during the Cromwellian wars,

St Columba's churchyard, Kells

No longer producing its famous whiskey, Locke's Distillery is now a museum

and is still there (see page 41). A copy can be seen at the Church of Ireland (St Columba's) in Kells.
Kells, 16km northwest of Navan.

NEWGRANGE
See Boyne Valley Archaeological Site (opposite).

SLANE HILL
It was here in 433, tradition has it, that St Patrick proclaimed the arrival of Christianity. The hill provides a splendid view of the Boyne Valley in fine weather.
13km west of Drogheda.

CO WESTMEATH
ATHLONE CASTLE
The Anglo-Norman castle was a military post from its erection in the 13th century until 1969, when it was declared

a National Monument controlled by the Office of Public Works. The Visitor Centre, with its museum and audio-visual display, opened in 1991 to mark the tercentenary of the Siege of Athlone. There is a folk and military museum in the keep, with relics of the town and district's history.
St Peter's Square, Athlone. Tel: 0902–92912. Open: May to September, daily 10am–5.15pm. Admission charge.

LOCKE'S DISTILLERY MUSEUM
Founded in 1757 and operational until 1953, this distillery, on the River Brosna, has been restored as an industrial museum and craft enterprise centre.
Kilbeggan, on the Dublin to Galway road (N6). Tel: 0506–32134. Open: April to October, daily 9am–6pm (reduced hours in winter). Admission charge.

Ireland's is a landscape of fantasy. Every scene, it seems – on mountainside, river bank or rocky shore – bears an exclamation mark of history in the form of a round tower or ruined castle.

Close your eyes and it is not difficult to conjure up figures from the past: hooded monks sprinting across the turf and pulling up the ladders against another gang of Viking raiders; minstrels making music while the lords and ladies feast; silhouettes flitting among flames as dark deeds are committed.

TOWERS

The 70 or so pencil-shaped round towers – unique to Ireland – which survive throughout the country date mainly from the ninth century. Built near ecclesiastical sites, especially monasteries, they served as belltowers, storehouses and watch-towers.

Varying in height from 15 to 45m, and usually tapering towards a stone cone-shaped top, the towers had a door set high enough above the ground to require a ladder for entry. This could be hauled in during an attack. Most towers originally had a number of floors reached by ladders and trapdoors, but some, probably used only as watch-towers, had a stairway. Among the best-preserved towers are those at Ardmore, Co Waterford; Cashel, Co Tipperary; Cloyne, Co Cork; Devenish Island, Co Fermanagh; Glendalough, Co Wicklow; and Monasterboice, Co Louth.

TOWERS AND CASTLES

CASTLES

The first stone castles – the earliest were timber constructions – were built by Norman colonists between 1190 and 1215. The grandest were those in Dublin, Kilkenny and Limerick.

Many of Ireland's castles date from a 15th-century building boom among such influential families as the MacCarthys (Blarney, Co Cork), the MacConmaras (Bunratty, Co Clare) and the MacNamaras (Knappogue, Co Clare). Bunratty and Knappogue are best known now for hosting medieval banquets.

Above left: Kildare Cathedral's 10th-century round tower
Above: Kilkenny Castle, a blend of Gothic and classical styles

Left: Carrickfergus Castle was built on its rocky promontory by John de Courcy in the late 12th century

CO LONGFORD
CARRIGGLAS MANOR

Built in 1837, this fine Victorian country house is home to the Lefroy family and contains many original furnishings. The stableyards house a costume and lace museum, and were designed by James Gandon, architect of the famous Custom House in Dublin. *8km from Longford, on the R194. Tel: 043–45165. Open: May and September, Monday, Friday 10.30am–3pm; June to August, Monday, Tuesday and Friday 10.30am–5pm, Sunday 2–6pm. Admission charge.*

CO OFFALY
BIRR CASTLE DEMESNE

Home of the Earls of Rosse, the castle is not open to the public, but the beautiful 40-hectare gardens are. Plants from remote parts of the world grow in these gardens, famous for the world's highest box hedge (10m), and for the permanent exhibition of the Rosse telescope, the world's largest when it was built in the mid-19th century. *Birr. Tel: 0509–20336. Open: daily 9am–6pm. Admission charge.*

Birr Castle, an impressive fortified manor house set in extensive grounds

BLACKWATER BOG TOUR

Organised by Bord Na Móna (the Irish Peat Board), this is a 9km tour of the Blackwater Bog aboard a Clonmacnoise & West Offaly Railway train. Visitors can learn of the 12,000-year development of the bog from glacier to lake, to fen and to bog. *Blackwater Works, Shannonbridge. Tel: 0905–74114. Open: April to October, Monday to Saturday 10am–5pm (tours on the hour), Sunday noon–5pm. Other times of the year by arrangement. Admission charge.*

CLONMACNOIS

One of Ireland's most sacred sites, and former burial place of the kings of Connacht and Tara, this monastic settlement, founded by St Ciarán in AD545, contains two round towers, the remains of a cathedral, nine church ruins, three high crosses, a 13th-century castle and over 200 grave slabs. The Nuns' Chapel and the 10th-century Cross of the Scriptures are particularly noted for the

quality of the mason's craft.
*Shannonbridge. Tel: 0905–74195. Open:
mid-March to October, daily 10am–6pm
(mid-May to September 9am–7pm);
November to mid-March, daily
10am–5.30pm. Admission charge.*

CO KILDARE
CASTLETOWN HOUSE
Ireland's first, and most important,
Palladian mansion was built in the
1720s for William Conolly, Speaker of
the Irish House of Commons. Its elegant
interior includes fine examples of 18th-
century furniture and superb plasterwork by the Francini brothers.
*Celbridge. Tel: 01–628 8252. Open: April
and May, Sunday and public holidays
1–6pm; June to September, Monday to
Friday 10am–6pm, Saturday, Sunday and
public holidays 1–6pm; October, Monday
to Friday 10am–5pm, Sunday and public
holidays 1–5pm; November, Sunday
1–5pm. Admission charge.*

JAPANESE GARDENS
These superb gardens at the Irish
National Stud, designed in 1906 for Lord
Wavertree, are thought by many to be the
finest in Europe; their design symbolises
the life-cycle of Man. St Fiachras Garden
is a new area that has been specially laid
out to celebrate the millennium.
*Tully, 1.5km south of Kildare town. Tel:
045–521617. Open: mid-February to mid-
November, 9.30am–6pm. Admission charge.*

STEAM MUSEUM
This model railway collection depicts
the development of the Irish locomotive
since the 18th century. Also on display
are full-size stationary steam engines.
*Lodge Park, Straffan. Tel: 01–627 3155.
Open: June to September, Tuesday to
Sunday and public holidays 2–6pm.
Admission charge.*

The Japanese Gardens, laid out by Japanese
gardener Eida, and his son Minoru

CO LAOIS
EMO COURT AND GARDENS
Possibly the premier attraction in the county, this fine Georgian mansion was designed by James Gandon, architect of Dublin's Custom House. Its great rotunda is lit by a lantern in the dome. The gardens contain fine statuary, rare trees, an imposing lake, shrubs and avenues of yews.
Emo. Tel: 0502–26573/21450. House open: mid-June to mid-September, Tuesday to Sunday, 10.30am–5pm (guided tours only); gardens, daily dawn to dusk. Admission charge to house; gardens free.

STEAM AND VINTAGE MACHINERY MUSEUM
Steam road engines and rollers operate here during traction engine rallies and railway events, with rides on Irish Peat Board loco-hauled coaches on narrow gauge railway, while displays portray the progress of steam in Ireland.
Irish Steam Preservation Society, The Green, Stradbally. Tel: 0502–25114/25444. Open: for rallies. Admission charge.

WINDY GAP
The Carlow to Stradbally road (N8) passes through Windy Gap, one of Ireland's most famous scenic drives. Stop at the Windy Gap car park for a long look over the Barrow Valley, with its wide vistas of the surrounding countryside.

CO CARLOW
ALTAMONT GARDENS
These fine gardens were planted in 1850, with a lily pool, arboretum, and a bog garden.
Off the N80 and N81, Tullow. Tel: 0503–59128/59444. Open: phone for times. Admission charge.

Ruins at the tiny hamlet of Avoca

BROWNE'S HILL DOLMEN
This impressive dolmen, which dates from around 2500BC, has the largest capstone in Ireland, and may even be the largest in Europe, estimated to weigh more than 101 tonnes. The front end of the capstone is supported by three uprights, while the rear has collapsed and rests on the ground.
Rathvilly Road, Carlow. Freely accessible (a path leads from the parking area).

CARLOW CASTLE
Carlow's ruined 13th-century castle has witnessed much bloodshed throughout its turbulent history. The castle survived attack from Cromwell's forces in the 17th century, but was badly damaged 150 years later during attempts to reduce the thickness of the walls using explosives. These ancient fortifications can be found on the east bank of the River Barrow in Carlow.
Freely accessible.

CO WICKLOW

AVOCA

The little village of Avoca is set in its picturesque valley, where the confluence of two rivers, the Avonbeg and the Avonmore inspired Thomas Moore to write his famous poem *The Meeting of the Waters* in 1807. The oldest hand-weaving mill in Ireland, Avoca Hand-weavers, still produces textiles in the traditional way and welcomes visitors.
4km south of Avondale. Handweavers – tel: 01-286 7466. Open: daily 9.30am–6pm. Free.

AVONDALE HOUSE

Avondale is the restored home of the nationalist leader, Charles Stewart Parnell (1846–91). Part of the house is devoted to a museum.
Rathdrum. Tel: 0404-46111. Open: Easter to December, Monday to Saturday 11am–6pm, Sunday 1–6pm. Admission charge.

GLENDALOUGH

Glendalough is the setting of Ireland's most important early Christian settlement, founded by St Kevin in the 6th century. It grew into a centre of learning and its fame spread throughout Europe. Visitors to the ancient ruin site can see a near-perfect round tower, a church with fine Irish Romanesque decoration, an oratory (St Kevin's Kitchen) and a 10th-century cathedral. A Visitor Centre houses an exhibition and audio-visual show.
16km west of Wicklow. Visitor Centre tel: 0404–45325. Open: mid-March to October, 9.30am–6pm (extended hours in summer); closes 5pm in winter. Site freely accessible. Admission charge for Visitor Centre.

MOUNT USHER GARDENS

Mount Usher is one of the finest examples of a 'wild garden', planted along the banks of the River Vartry. Laid out in 1868, it contains rare trees, shrubs and flowers from all over the world, including 70 species of eucalyptus.
Ashford, on the main Dublin/Rosslare road. Tel: 0404–40116. Open: mid-March to early November, daily 10.30am–6pm. Admission charge.

The gardens at Mount Usher are set along the banks of its winding stream

POWERSCOURT GARDENS

The main block of this Palladian-style house was gutted by fire in 1974, but an exhibition of photographs shows its former glory. The gardens however, live on. They include English, Italian and Japanese sections and are rich in sculptures, a fountain and terraces, formal flower beds and conifers. Some 5km away is spectacular Powerscourt Waterfall, at 120m the highest in Ireland.
Enniskerry, near Bray. Tel: 01–204 6000. Open: daily 9.30am–5.30pm (winter times may vary). Separate admission charges for exhibition/gardens/waterfall.

Powerscourt, one of Ireland's great gardens, uses ornamental features to good effect

RUSSBOROUGH HOUSE

This mid-18th-century mansion with its sumptuous plasterwork is home to the Beit Collection of paintings, which includes works by Gainsborough, Murillo and Velázquez. The rhododendron garden·is open in late spring.
Blessington. Tel: 045–865239. Open: June to August, daily 10.30am–5pm (to 2.30pm weekdays May and September); spring and autumn reduced hours. Admission charge.

CO KILKENNY

DUNMORE CAVE

The human bones and coins that have been found in this natural limestone cavern, suggest that Vikings may have caused the deaths of many people, including children, in 928.

Well-lit walkways lead through the cave, illuminating enormous stalagmite and stalactite formations, and a small centre explains the history and geology of the cave system.
Ballyfoyle, 11km north of Kilkenny off the N78. Tel: 056–67726. Open: mid-March to October, daily 10am–5pm (extended hours in summer); weekends and public holidays only in winter. Guided tours only. Admission charge.

JERPOINT ABBEY

This 12th-century Cistercian abbey is one of Ireland's finest monastic ruins. The abbey's extensive remains are awe-inspiring, and it has particularly fine, detailed carvings in the cloisters.
3.5km south of Thomastown, on the N9. Tel: 056–24623. Open: March to October, daily 10am–5pm (extended hours in summer); November, daily 10am–4pm. Last admission 45 minutes before closing. Admission charge.

KILKENNY CASTLE

Set above the waters of the River Nore, imposing 12th-century Kilkenny Castle, remodelled in Victorian times, is noted for its restored great hall and extensive art gallery.
The Parade, Kilkenny. Tel: 056–21450. Open: April and May, daily 10.30am–5pm; June to September, daily 10am–7pm; October to March, Tuesday to Saturday 10.30am, 12.45pm, 2–5pm, Sunday 11am–12.45pm, 2–5pm. Guided tours only. Admission charge.

ROTHE HOUSE

A charming example of a 16th-century Town House with a fine art collection and exhibition of period costumes.
Parliament Street, Kilkenny. Tel: 056–22893. Open: Monday to Saturday, 1–5pm, Sunday 3–5pm (longer hours in summer). Admission charge.

ST CANICE'S CATHEDRAL

Renowned for its grandeur, carvings and marble monuments, St Canice's Cathedral was built in the 13th century. The nearby 9th-century round tower can be climbed, weather permitting.
Irishtown, Kilkenny. Tel: 056–64971. Open: Monday to Saturday 9am–1pm, 2–6pm (10am–1pm, 2–4pm October to April), Sunday 2–6pm (to 4pm October to April). Donation requested for round tower.

CO WEXFORD

IRISH NATIONAL HERITAGE PARK

This excellent, open-air site is a good introduction to Ireland, from prehistoric to medieval times, including authentic reconstructions of Stone-Age and Bronze-Age fortifications and settlements and a Norman motte and bailey.
Ferrycarrig. Tel: 053–20733. Open: March to November, daily 9.30am–6.30pm (last admission 5pm). Times may be subject to seasonal change. Admission charge.

JOHN F KENNEDY ARBORETUM

Situated above the Kennedy Homestead, this collection of 4,500 types of trees and shrubs is set in 252 hectares. In summer, visitors can tour it by pony and trap or miniature railway.
Dunganstown, New Ross. Tel: 051–388171. Open: daily from 10am (to 6.30pm April and September, to 8pm May to August, to 5pm October to March). Admission charge.

After its dissolution in 1540, Jerpoint Abbey was granted to the Ormonde family

WESTGATE HERITAGE CENTRE

An audio-visual presentation of the town's early history is appropriately set in an early 13th-century gate tower which forms part of the town's original Viking/Norman walls.
Selskar Abbey, Wexford. Tel: 053–46506. Open: Monday to Friday 9.30am–4pm, weekends 10.30am–4pm. Admission charge.

WEXFORD WILDFOWL RESERVE

Bewick swans, white-fronted geese, pintails, gulls and other species winter on the mudflats of this wildlife reserve on the Slaney Estuary. The reserve also has many walks, an observation tower, hides, a visitor centre and wildfowl identification charts.
North Sloblands. Tel: 053–23129. Open: April to September, daily 9am–6pm; October to March, daily 10am–5pm. Free.

Dublin's Old City

This area has witnessed the Dublin story from its very beginnings. Here, the Vikings settled in 841. Some 300 years later, Strongbow stormed the city, and a castle was built. *Allow 1½ hours.*

Begin on Wellington Quay with Ha'penny Bridge behind you and head south.

1 TEMPLE BAR AREA

This maze of narrow streets has developed into an arty area of bistros, boutiques and art galleries, all tucked into the ageing warehouses formally occupied by merchants and craftsmen. *Head west (right) along Temple Bar, then turn left into Temple Lane and continue to Dame Street.*

2 DAME STREET

Near by

4 Marsh's Library (see page 31)

Dame Street once provided access to the nunnery of St Mary del Dame, but its name derives from a dam once built on the River Poddle, now running underground. Dublin's oldest surviving theatre, the Olympia, was opened here in 1870. *Turn left into Castle Street. Ahead is the gate to Upper Castle Yard.*

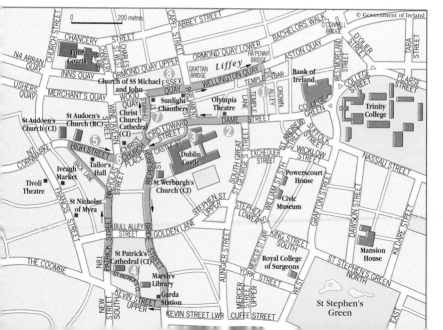

3 DUBLIN CASTLE

Work on the castle began in 1205, although there are indications that defensive earthworks existed before the Vikings arrived. Guided tours of the castle and State Apartments are normally available (see page 26).
Leave by the Justice Gate. Continue left along Castle Street; turn left into Werburgh and Bride streets. After turning right into Kevin Street Upper, turn right again into St Patrick's Close.

4 ST PATRICK'S CATHEDRAL

Standing on a site traditionally associated with Ireland's patron saint, St Patrick's Cathedral dates from 1191. A bust of Jonathan Swift, author of *Gulliver's Travels*, is at the west end of the nave (see page 39).
Turn right into Patrick Street, left into Back Lane and right into High Street.

5 HIGH STREET

The Tailor's Hall in Back Lane, built around 1706, is Dublin's last surviving Guild Hall. The 'Back Lane Parliament' met here in 1792. St Audoen's, the city's oldest surviving medieval parish church, has a 12th-century tower, 15th-century nave and a font dating from 1194. The 'Flame on the Hill' audio-visual presentation in neighbouring St Audoen's Roman Catholic Church, tells the story of life in pre-Viking Ireland (see page 38).
Cross Nicholas Street/Winetavern Street to Christ Church Place.

6 CHRIST CHURCH PLACE

Built in the mid-11th century and re-built in stone by the Anglo-Normans, Christ Church Cathedral contains the tomb of Strongbow, Earl of Pembroke (see page 24).

Twelfth-century Christ Church Cathedral replaced a timber-built church

Bear left along Christ Church Place to Fishamble Street.

7 FISHAMBLE STREET

This was the home of Dublin's fish market before becoming fashionable. It was the birthplace of Archbishop Ussher, the poet James Clarence Mangan and the nationalist Henry Grattan, and witnessed the first performance of Handel's *Messiah*.
At the river turn right into Essex Quay.

8 ESSEX QUAY

At the western end of Essex Quay, the Franciscan church of SS Michael and John incorporates the remains of the Smock-Alley Theatre, built in 1661 and closed in the 1790s when the gallery collapsed during a performance. At the eastern end, Sunlight Chambers, built around 1900, has an ornate terracotta frieze illustrating the manufacture and uses of soap.
Cross Parliament Street and continue along Wellington Quay to end the walk back at Ha'penny Bridge.

NORTHERN IRELAND
Enniskillen · Belfast
Sligo·
Galway· REPUBLIC
OF · Dublin
Limerick IRELAND
Killarney Waterford
Cork·

Dublin's Cultural Heart

Dublin north of the Liffey is the city's cultural heart. Here are the widest and largest streets, the best Georgian houses and the most splendid public buildings. Here also are the Abbey and Gate theatres. *Allow 2 hours.*

Begin on the north side of O'Connell Bridge, following Eden Quay to Custom House Quay.

1 CUSTOM HOUSE

Dublin's most magnificent building, Custom House was designed by James Gandon. Since its opening in 1792, it has survived three major fires – the last, in 1921, was so fierce that brass fittings melted (see page 26).
Return to Butt Bridge, then turn right into Beresford Place.

Near by

4 Hugh Lane Municipal Gallery of Modern Art

2 ABBEY STREET

The Abbey Theatre, on the corner of Marlborough Street, was founded in 1904 by a group led by W B Yeats (see page 24).

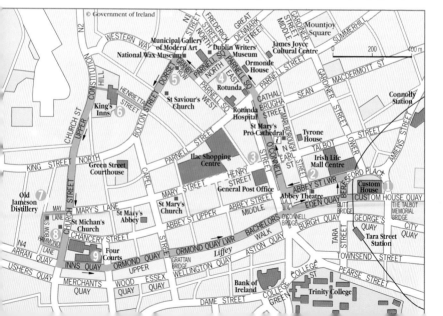

Opposite are the offices of the National Lottery, instituted to provide funds for the arts, culture and sport.
Turn right into O'Connell Street.

3 O'CONNELL STREET

O'Connell Street is one of the world's great thoroughfares. It is dominated by the Georgian majesty of the General Post Office, which was shelled and set ablaze when it became headquarters of the Irish Volunteers in the Easter Rising of 1916 (see page 27). O'Connell Street has many associations with Ireland's struggle for independence.

The statue of a gigantic maiden lying in the running waters of a stream, in the central mall, is the Anna Livia Millennium Fountain, symbolising the spirit of the Liffey – Dubliners call it 'the Floozie in the Jacuzzi'.
Cross Parnell Street to Parnell Square East.

4 PARNELL SQUARE

Originally known as the Barley Fields, Parnell Square dates from 1748 when it was laid out as pleasure gardens. On the left, beyond the monument to Charles Stewart Parnell, is the Gate Theatre, built in 1786 and converted to a theatre in 1930. Parnell Square North houses the Dublin Writers' Museum (see pages 26–7).
Turn right into Granby Row.

5 GRANBY ROW

Granby Row was the work of the Georgian developer Luke Gardiner, who had a profound influence throughout the city. The National Wax Museum is located on the corner with Dorset Street (see page 33).
Turn left into Dorset Street. Continue along Bolton Street and turn right into Henrietta Street.

6 HENRIETTA STREET

Another Gardiner development, this was once the most fashionable street in Dublin, housing at one time in the mid-18th century five peers, a peeress, a peer's son, a judge, a Member of Parliament, a bishop and two wealthy clergymen.
At the end of Henrietta Street pass through the central arch of King's Inns and cross the park to Constitution Hill. Turning left, continue to Church Street. Turn right into May Lane.

7 OLD JAMESON DISTILLERY

Visitors get the chance to taste some different blends of Irish whiskey in this museum for adults. The museum can be found in what was the Old Jameson Distillery (see page 33).
Turn left on to Bow Street and left again along Hammond Lane to Church Street.

8 ST MICHAN'S CHURCH

St Michan's contains a magnificent organ on which Handel is believed to have played. It also has a Penitent's Stool and a 16th-century chalice. But the church is best known for its limestone vaults where mummified bodies are on view (see page 38).
Head south along Church Street, turning left on to Inns Quay.

9 FOUR COURTS

Designed by Gandon and completed in 1802, the massive Georgian edifice confronting the Liffey is the seat of the Irish Law Courts. Columns of the portico still bear battle scars inflicted in 1922 when the building was shelled during the civil war (see page 27).
Continue parallel to the Liffey along Ormond Quay and complete the walk back at O'Connell Bridge.

Munster

*A*s well as Co Tipperary, Ireland's largest inland county, Munster contains the counties of Waterford, Cork, Kerry, Limerick and Clare. Its terrain is as varied as Ireland itself, from the Golden Plain of Tipperary to the rugged coastlines of Cork, the mountains of Kerry and the majestic Cliffs of Moher in Clare. Here, the past and present merge. The ancient ringforts and dolmens and the mystic Rock of Cashel share the province with three of Ireland's largest industrial cities: Cork, Limerick and Waterford.

CO TIPPERARY
BOLTON LIBRARY
A fine collection of illuminated manuscripts, books and maps. Exhibitions of printing, antique books and silver are frequently staged.
Grounds of St John the Baptist Cathedral, Cashel. Tel: 062–61232. Open: May to September, Tuesday to Friday 10am–6pm (weekend appointments). Admission charge.

Cashel's excellent Folk Village portrays rural life

BRÚ BORÚ HERITAGE CENTRE
Named after BrianBorú, the 11th-century High King of Ireland, this cultural village incorporates a folk theatre, craft centre, information centre and a computerised genealogy service. Music, drama and banquets are held from Tuesday to Saturday evenings throughout the summer, and the restaurant serves Irish fare.
Near the Rock of Cashel. Tel: 062–61122. Open: mid-June to mid-September, daily 9am–late; rest of year, Monday to Friday 9am–5pm (to 2pm Friday, November to Easter). Evening performances. Free.

CAHIR CASTLE
Built on a rocky island in the middle of the River Suir, Cahir Castle, one of the best preserved in Ireland, has been impressively restored. Built in the 15th and 16th centuries, its oldest parts date from 1164. Furnishings are authentic reproductions of the period. Scenes for the films *Excalibur* and *Barry Lyndon* were shot here, and there are guided tours. An audio-visual presentation highlights the area's antiquities.
Cahir. Tel: 052–641011. Open: mid-March to mid-June and mid-September to mid-October, daily 9.30am–5.30pm; mid-June to mid-September, daily 9am–7.30pm; mid-October to mid-March, daily 9.30am–1pm, 2–4.30pm. Admission charge.

MUNSTER

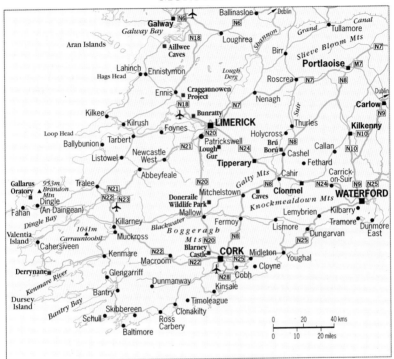

CASHEL FOLK VILLAGE

Cashel's Folk Village is an interesting collection of reconstructed houses and shops displaying furniture, artefacts and tools portraying local life from the 18th to 20th centuries.

Dominick Street, Cashel. Tel: 062–62525. Open: March and April, daily 10am–6pm; May to October, daily 9.30am–7.30pm. Admission charge.

CASHEL HERITAGE CENTRE

The story of the Kings of Cashel from AD300 is featured in Cashel's Heritage Centre. Tram rides in summer.

Main Street, Cashel. Tel: 062–62511. Open: daily 9.30am–5.30pm (extended hours in summer). Admission charge.

FETHARD FOLK, FARM AND TRANSPORT MUSEUM

More than 2,500 items arranged in a series of 'real-life' reconstructions are displayed in the freight depot of an old railway station. Major features include a forge, a country kitchen, a jaunting car, a baker's van and a horse-drawn hearse.

Cashel Road, Fethard. Tel: 052–31516. Open: Sunday 12.30–5pm. Admission charge.

HOLY CROSS ABBEY

Founded in 1180, left derelict for 400 years and restored totally between 1971 and 1985, the abbey thrives as a parish church. It incorporates architecture of the 12th and 15th centuries, with excellent stone carvings and window traceries. *Holycross, 6km south of Thurles, on the R660. Tel: 0504–43241. Open: daily. Donation appreciated.*

Detail of stone carving at the Rock of Cashel

MITCHELSTOWN CAVE

Visitors can take an escorted tour through the spectacular rock formations of these massive, high-ceilinged chambers, only discovered in recent times. *Burncourt, midway between Cahir and Mitchelstown. Tel: 052–67246. Open: daily 10am–5pm (to 6pm April to October). Admission charge.*

NENAGH HERITAGE CENTRE

Nenagh's former county gaol houses the town's Heritage Centre. It features the excellent Lifestyles in Northwest Tipperary Exhibition and there are frequent temporary displays of paintings and photographs. *Opposite the Castle Keep, Nenagh. Tel: 067–32633. Open: mid-May to October,*

Monday to Friday 10am–5pm, weekends 2.30–5pm. Admission charge.

ORMONDE CASTLE

Ireland's best example of a fortified Elizabethan manor house, Ormonde Castle was built in 1560s alongside an older building overlooking the River Suir. It is said to have been built by the Earl of Ormonde, to entertain Queen Elizabeth I, who never arrived. The older castle is said to be the birthplace of Anne Boleyn, wife of Henry VIII. *Castle Park, Carrick-on-Suir. Tel: 051–640787. Open: mid-June to September, daily 9.30am–6.30pm. Guided tours only. Admission charge.*

ROCK OF CASHEL

The Rock of Cashel – the Gaelic word means 'stone fort' – soars 60m above the Golden Vale. Legend has it that the Devil took a bite out of the nearby Slieve Bloom Mountains and spat it out on to the plains when he was surprised by St Patrick.

Crowning the rock is a wealth of medieval architecture. The oldest building, the Round Tower, is thought to date from the 10th century, but it is certain that the site was hallowed in pre-Christian times. The High Kings of Munster are said to have been crowned on the summit.

Cormac's Chapel, completed in 1134, is the best-preserved of the Rock's buildings and is also the earliest of Ireland's surviving Romanesque churches. It was built by Cormac MacCarthy, King of Desmond and Bishop of Cashel, and its twisted columns, steeply-pitched roof and fine carvings contribute to its unique beauty.

St Patrick's Cathedral, the largest building, was built about a century later than the chapel. The 13th-century building was burned down in 1495 and restored in the 16th century. The Apostles and scenes from the Apocalypse are represented in sculptures in the north transept, and there is a splendid view of the surrounding vale from the top of the central tower.

The Hall of Vicars is the first building to be reached by those approaching the Rock from Cashel town. It was built in the 15th century for eight vicars who assisted in the cathedral services. On the ground floor is the original St Patrick's Cross (the one outside is a replica), a high cross less ornately carved than usual.
Cashel. Tel: 062–61437. Open: mid-March to mid-June, daily 9.30am–5.30pm; mid-June to mid-September, daily 9am–7.30pm; mid-September to mid-March, daily 9.30am–4.30pm. (Last admission 45 minutes before closing.) Admission charge.

TIPPERARY COUNTY MUSEUM
This permanent display of 19th- and early 20th-century items of political, civic and industrial interest also has frequent exhibitions staged in association with the National Museum and Library.
Municipal Library, Parnell Street, Clonmel. Tel: 052–25399. Museum will close late 1999 to move to new premises.

Rock of Cashel, stronghold of the kings of Munster for over 700 years

Christ Church Cathedral, Waterford, built to the same plan as Dublin's Christ Church

CO WATERFORD
ARDMORE MONASTIC SITE
According to legend, 30 years before St Patrick arrived in Ireland in the 5th century, St Declan crossed from Wales and established a monastic settlement at Ardmore. He chose a magnificent location, affording stunning views over the bay, and as a result of his arrival the area surrounding the site is known to this day as Old Parish – believed to be the oldest parish in Ireland.

The site of the saint's original monastic foundation is today marked by an exceptionally well-preserved 11th-century round tower in the ruined Cathedral of St Declan. The surrounding graveyard, pitching steeply towards the coast, contains St Declan's

Oratory, where the saint is believed to be buried. Roofless though it is, the old cathedral is an evocative place, especially when one views the strikingly carved murals depicting the *Adoration of the Magi*, the *Fall of Man*, the *Judgement of Solomon* and the *Weighing of Souls*. *Signposted off the N25 between Dungarvan, (Co Waterford) and Youghal (Co Cork). Freely accessible.*

CHRIST CHURCH CATHEDRAL
Designed by John Roberts, a Waterford architect whose work included the city's Holy Trinity Cathedral, Christ Church is an ornate Renaissance-style structure built in the 1770s to replace a church which had stood on the site since the 11th century. Standing in a pleasant square, the Church of Ireland cathedral contains interesting monuments, including the 15th-century tomb of James Rice, depicting a decaying corpse.

Across the square from the cathedral is the roofless French Church, founded as a Franciscan friary in 1240 and later used by Huguenot refugees. It has a fine east window and the tomb of Sir Neal O'Neill, who fled with James II after the Battle of the Boyne. *Cathedral Square, Waterford. Tel: 051–858958. Open: May to September, daily (key from Heritage Museum, Greyfriars). Donation expected.*

CURRAGHMORE
This house has been the ancestral home of Lord Waterford and his forebears since 1170. Detailed plasterwork is a feature of the interior.

The beautiful grounds surrounding Curraghmore contain a fine example of an Arboretum, an 18th-century shell grotto (designed and built by the Countess of Tyrone) and a 13th-century

bridge which spans the River Clogagh.
Portlaw, Co Waterford. Tel: 051–387102.
Grounds and shell house open: Easter to mid-
October, Thursday and Bank Holidays
2–5pm. House tours Jan, May and June.
Admission charge.

HOLY TRINITY CATHEDRAL
The simple exterior of Waterford's
Roman Catholic cathedral, also designed
by John Roberts, conceals an
extravagantly decorated interior hung
with chandeliers of Waterford crystal.
Barronstrand Street, Waterford. Freely
accessible.

LISMORE CASTLE GARDENS
One of several places linked with
Edmund Spenser's poem *The Faerie*
Queene, the gardens have a fine collection
of shrubs, including camellias and
magnolias, and restful woodland walks.
A dramatic yew walk is believed to be
more than 800 years old. The Irish home
of the Dukes of Devonshire, the estate
was once leased to Sir Walter Raleigh.
The present castle, built in the mid-19th
century, is not open to the public.

Right: Lismore Heritage Centre relates the
town's long and varied history
Below: spectacularly lit Lismore Castle

Signposted in Lismore. Tel: 058–54424.
Open: Garden tours – late April to late
September, daily 1.45–4.45pm. Admission
charge.

LISMORE HERITAGE CENTRE
Lismore has a rich history: founded as a
monastic centre in AD636, it became a
famous seat of learning, was sacked
repeatedly by Vikings and Normans,
and became involved in many religious
and political struggles. The story is told
in an audio-visual presentation.
The Courthouse, Lismore. Tel: 058–54975.
Open: Monday to Friday 9.30am–5.30pm;
April to October also Sunday 10am–5.30pm
(Saturdays in summer). Admission charge
includes guided tour of the town Monday to
Saturday 11.30am and 3pm.

REGINALD'S TOWER MUSEUM

Originally built by the Vikings in 1003 (the present structure dates from the 12th century), as part of Waterford's defences, the squat but massive tower has walls 3m thick and stands 25m high. In its time it has served as a royal residence, a mint, a gaol and an arsenal.
The Quay, Waterford. Tel: 051–873501. Open: April to October, daily 10am–5pm (to 8.30pm in summer). Admission charge.

Reginald's Tower takes its name from Ragnvald the Dane, who supposedly built it

WATERFORD CITY HALL

This fine Georgian building dates from 1783 and incorporates the Theatre Royal, where the city's International Light Opera Festival is staged every September. A huge Waterford glass chandelier, made in 1802, hangs in the council chamber (a copy can be found in Philadelphia's Independence Hall). The uniform and sword of Thomas Francis Meagher, a Waterford man who fought in the Irish Brigade at Fredericksburg in the American Civil War, is included in a collection of military memorabilia.
The Mall, Waterford. Tel: 051–873501. Open: Monday to Friday 10am–5pm. Free.

WATERFORD CRYSTAL

Tours of the famous factory include an audio-visual presentation on the history of glassmaking. Examples of Waterford Crystal can be seen in the gallery display area afterwards.
Cork Road, Kilbarry, 1.5km from Waterford, on the N25. Tel: 051–873311. Open: April to October, daily 8.30am–6pm, tours to 4pm (5pm in winter, tours to 3.15pm). Gallery open weekends in winter, except January. Tour charge; gallery free.

WATERFORD HERITAGE MUSEUM

Viking and Norman artefacts unearthed during extensive excavations in the city in the 1980s are displayed in a former 19th-century church. The exhibition – only a selection of some of the 75,000 items uncovered – includes leatherware, pottery and jewellery.
Greyfriars Street, Waterford. Tel: 051–871227. Open: daily 10am–5pm (closed weekends in winter).

WATERFORD TREASURES

Opened in 1999, this old granary houses treasures relating to all aspects of Waterfords colourful history.
The Granary, Waterford. Tel: 051–304500 Open: daily 9.30am–9pm (extended hours in summer). Admission charge.

CO CORK
BANTRY HOUSE

Exquisitely set in Italianate gardens overlooking the magnificent bay, this Georgian mansion dates from around

Intricate detail being engraved on a fine
example of Waterford Crystal

1740. There are extensive collections of
art and antiques, including a tapestry
made for Marie-Antoinette. The French
Armada Interpretive Centre, also
located here, contains documents,
weapons and artefacts from a ship which
sank during the French invasion attempt
of 1796.
*Outskirts of Bantry. Tel: 027–50047.
Open: March to October, daily 9am–6pm
(to 8pm in summer). Admission charge.*

BLARNEY CASTLE

Built around 1446, the castle was the
stronghold of the MacCarthys, and it
was Dermot MacCarthy, Lord Blarney,
whose smooth talk and empty promises
exasperated Elizabeth I and brought a
new word into the English language.
To acquire this 'gift of the gab'
(eloquence), visitors must first climb
over 120 steps, then lie on their back,
hang over an open space and kiss the
legendary Blarney Stone. The central
keep, all that remains of the old castle, is
set in pleasantly landscaped gardens and

there are good views of the surrounding
Lee Valley.
*8km northwest of Cork on the R617. Tel:
021–385252. Open: May to September,
Monday to Saturday 9am–7pm (to 8.30pm
in June and July), Sunday
9.30am–5.30pm; off-season, Sunday
9.30am–sunset. Admission charge.*

CHARLES FORT

Built in the late 17th century after the
defeat of the Spanish and Irish in the
Battle of Kinsale, this is one of Europe's
most complete star forts (so-called
because of its shape). Covering some 5
hectares on a clifftop site, it was
occupied by British troops until 1920.
*Summer Cove, 3km east of Kinsale. Tel:
021–772263. Open: mid-March to October,
daily 10am–6pm; November to mid-March,
weekends 10am–5pm (weekdays by
arrangement). Admission charge.*

Braving the dizzying height to kiss the
legendary Blarney Stone

FLORA AND FAUNA

Ireland preserves natural habitats which have disappeared from the rest of Europe. Naturalists from all over the world visit unique locations like The Burren to see Arctic and Mediterranean plants growing side by side. They travel to rocky islands, rich wetlands and areas still farmed traditionally to observe huge concentrations of migratory birds and species that have become rare in other countries – like the corncrake and the chough.

You are never far from the countryside in Ireland. A well-marked 3km nature trail is within 3km of Belfast city centre – at Lagan Meadows, starting at the Knightsbridge Park entrance. Here you can see kingfishers, snipe, woodcocks, reed buntings and herons.

The National Trust has built several bird hides at Strangford Lough. Migrant geese, ducks, shorebirds and seabirds gather here by the thousands at different seasons (see page 103).

Rathlin Island, off the north coast, attracts serious ornithologists with its extensive sanctuary at Kebble. Huge numbers of birds sit wing to wing on cliff ledges and rock stacks, raucously shrieking – puffins, razorbills, fulmars, guillemots (see page 126).

Otters thrive all over Ireland. Native red deer, pine martens, red squirrels, grey seals, dolphins, wild goats and hares are among mammals regularly seen. There are no snakes, however – legend has it St Patrick drove them all out of Ireland.

Cape Clear, an island off Co Cork, has an observatory built by Bristol University from which rare songbird migrants are seen, as well as seabirds (see page 127).

The nutrient-poor boglands sustain many small plants – deer sedge, bog cotton, bog rosemary, bog asphodel – and insects. Sundews, butterworts and bladderworts trap insects for sustenance.

The Burren, in Co Clare, is a vast, waterless plateau of limestone hills, drawing geologists and botanists, especially in May, when countless colourful flowers appear.

Above left: wild
orchid

Left: characteristic
Burren landscape

Above: the Twelve
Bens (Pins), near
Roundstone

Left: sika deer
at Gortin

Drombeg stone circle is one of the best
preserved monuments of its kind in Ireland

DROMBEG STONE CIRCLE

The Cork-Kerry region has the highest
concentration of stone circles in Ireland,
and Drombeg Circle is one of the most
accessible. It stands in a small field with
a commanding sea view. An unusual
feature of Drombeg is its communal
cooking pit in which some 340 litres of
water could be boiled by throwing in hot
stones. A TV cook has successfully
cooked a joint of meat there, using the
Stone Age method.
3km west of Ross Carbery, on the R597,
which loops back on to the N71 just before
Leap. Freely accessible.

FOTA WILDLIFE PARK

Giraffes, kangaroos, oryx and monkeys
wander freely among penguins,
flamingos and peacocks, while an
informal arboretum features exotic trees
from all over the world. The 30-hectare
park specialises in the breeding of
certain endangered species.
Fota Island, Cork Harbour, 13km east of
Cork on the N25. Also reached by train
from Cork. Tel: 021- 812678. Open: April
to September, Monday to Saturday 10am–
6pm, Sunday 11am–6pm; rest of year
weekends only. Last admission 5.15pm.
Admission charge.

GARINISH ISLAND

Rare sub-tropical plants jostle with
rhododendrons, azaleas, climbing shrubs
and herbaceous perennials on this
colourful island in Bantry Bay, a
favourite with George Bernard Shaw.
The beautiful Italianate gardens, with
colonnades, pools and terraces, as well
as a wild garden, were laid out between
1810 and 1913.
Reached in 10 minutes by boat from
Glengarriff. Tel: 027–63040. Open: March
and October, Monday to Saturday 10am–
4.30pm, Sunday 1–5pm; April to June and
September, Monday to Saturday 10am–
6.30pm, Sunday 1–7pm (extended hours in
July and August). Last landing one hour
before closing. Ferry charge.

JAMESON HERITAGE CENTRE

The story of whiskey, the mystical spirit
perfected by Irish monks in the 6th
century, is told in the old stone buildings
of a distillery, complete with the
world's largest copper still, a cast-iron
mill wheel, traditional craft displays – and
a generous tot at the end of the tour.
Signposted from the N25 at Midleton,
19km east of Cork. Tel: 021–613594.
Open: tours – March to October, daily
9am–4.30pm; November to February,
weekday tours 12 and 3pm, weekend tours
2 and 4pm. Admission charge.

MYRTLE GROVE

Sir Walter Raleigh is said to have
smoked Ireland's first pipe of tobacco
and planted the first potatoes at Myrtle
Grove, one of the country's oldest
unfortified houses, when he was Warden
of Youghal in 1588–9. Edmund
Spenser, the poet, also stayed at the
gabled Elizabethan mansion.
Main Street, Youghal. Not accessible to the
public.

Garinish's Italian gardens: George Bernard Shaw wrote much of his *St Joan* here

FAMINE AND EMIGRATION

Cobh, formerly known as Queenstown, was the embarkation point for thousands of emigrants – many of them victims of the appalling famine years of 1845–8 when Ireland's potato crop repeatedly failed as a result of blight. Facing starvation, a million people left the country for good, seeking a new life in Australia, Canada, New Zealand and the United States, and setting up huge Irish communities overseas.

ST FINN BARRE'S CATHEDRAL

The 19th-century French Gothic cathedral, with its three spires, stands on the site of a 6th-century monastery founded by St Finbarr, who also founded Cork in the early part of the 7th century (see page 77).
Bishop Street, Cork. Open: daily 9am–6pm. Free.

St Finn Barre's Cathedral, belonging to the Church of Ireland, designed by William Burges

SHANDON STEEPLE

Dominating the skyline on the north side of the River Lee in Cork, the pepperpot steeple of St Anne's Church invites visitors to fill the city with music – those who climb the 37m structure can choose a tune to be played on the carillon.
Church Street, Shandon. Tel: 021–505906. Open: Monday to Friday 10am–5.30pm. Admission charge.

TIMOLEAGUE ABBEY AND CASTLE GARDENS

Set at the head of a long sea inlet, Timoleague Abbey was founded in 1240 and is one of Ireland's best-preserved early Franciscan friaries. Among the country's largest and most important religious houses, the monks here once traded as importers of Spanish wine.

Overlooking the abbey, palm trees and other exotic trees and shrubs flourish in beautiful walled gardens which embrace the scant ruins of 13th-century Timoleague Castle.

Signposted in the village of Timoleague. Abbey – freely accessible. Castle gardens – tel: 023–46116. Open: Easter weekend and mid-May to mid-September, daily noon–6pm. Admission charge.

The greystone ruins of Timoleague Abbey, once Ireland's largest friary

CO KERRY

DARRYNANE HOUSE AND NATIONAL HISTORIC PARK

The home of Daniel O'Connell, the 'Liberator', is now kept as a museum and memorial to the great 19th-century politician. The National Historic Park surrounding the house covers 120 hectares of sub-tropical plants, shrubs and coastal trees. There is also a nature trail, and visitors can bathe in the sea (see also **Cahersiveen** page 79).

Signposted off the N70, 1.5km north of Caherdaniel. Tel: 066–9475113. Open: April and October, Tuesday to Sunday 1–5pm; May to September, Monday to Saturday 9am–6pm, Sunday 11am–7pm (weekends 1–5pm in winter). Last admission 45 minutes before closing. Admission charge to house; grounds freely accessible.

DUNBEG FORT

Perched on a promontory high above Dingle Bay, this Iron Age fort is protected on its landward side by trenches and a 7m-thick wall. The circular fort itself, now ruined, also has thick walls.

On the R559 near Fahan, about 6km west of Ventry. Freely accessible.

GALLARUS ORATORY

Amazingly pristine, the oratory is a perfect example of early Irish building, dating from the 8th or possibly the 7th century. Completely unmortared, it has remained watertight for 1,200 years.

Off the R559, between Ballyferriter and Ballynana. Freely accessible.

KERRY THE KINGDOM

A 'time car' trip back to medieval Tralee, along a reconstructed street and into houses peopled with life-like models in

BEEHIVE HUTS

More than 400 *clochans* – beehive-shaped stone cells – are to be found on the southern slopes of Mount Eagle. Although unmortared, the prehistoric structures are quite watertight, and in early Christian times were used by hermit monks. The greatest concentration of huts is on the R559 between Slea Head and Dunquin, many in fields and farmyards.

Shaped like an upturned boat, Gallarus Oratory has stood the test of time

authentic dress. Incorporated in this attraction is the **Kerry County Museum**, which outlines 7,000 years of the area's history.
Ashe Memorial Hall, Denny Street, Tralee. Tel: 066–7127777. Open: March to October, daily 10am–6pm; November and December, noon–4.30pm. Admission charge.

KILMALKEDAR CHURCH

This ruined 12th-century church is a fine example of Romanesque architecture. The narrow east window is known locally as 'the eye of the needle' through which those seeking salvation must pass. The Alphabet Stone, a pillar standing inside the church, is inscribed with both Roman and ancient Irish characters.
Off the R559, near the Gallarus Oratory. Freely accessible.

MUCKROSS ABBEY AND HOUSE

Despite vandalism by Cromwell's troops in 1652, which left it roofless, the 15th-century Franciscan abbey remains in a surprisingly good state of preservation. Visitors can climb ancient stone stairs to examine the monks' living quarters, kitchen and refectory.

Not far from the abbey is Muckross House. Surrounded by landscaped gardens noted for rhododendrons and azaleas, it was built in the 19th century in Elizabethan style. Its upper floors house a collection of maps, prints and other documents and there is a small wildlife and bird exhibition. The house also incorporates the Kerry Folklife Centre with a country pub, print shop, dairy and carpenter's shop. Craftspeople demonstrate weaving, basket-making, pottery and smithying. Near by are Muckross Traditional Farms, three separate working farms with animals and an exhibition of traditional farm machinery.
On the N71 Kenmare road, 6km outside Killarney. Abbey open: daily during daylight hours. Free. House – tel: 064–31440. Open: daily 9am–6pm (to 7pm in July and August). Farms: March to October only. Admission charge for house and farms.

SKELLIG EXPERIENCE

This interpretative centre explores the history and archaeology of Skellig Michael's Early Christian monastery, its lighthouse service, and local wildlife.
Valentina Island, by road bridge from Portmagee. Tel: 066–9476306. Open: April to October, daily 10am–6pm (from 9.30am July and August). Admission charge.

CO LIMERICK

FOYNES FLYING BOAT MUSEUM

The focal point for aircraft crossing the north Atlantic in the 1930s and 1940s, the old terminus building, radio and weather rooms are on show, with original equipment. An audio-visual presentation is given in a 1940s-style cinema and there is a tea room of the same era.
On the N69, about 24km west of Limerick. Tel: 069–65416. Open: April to October, daily 10am–6pm. Admission charge.

KING JOHN'S CASTLE

Imaginative models and displays interpret Limerick's 800-year history in the city's restored 13th-century castle. Battlement walkways along the castle walls and towers provide wonderful views of the city, the River Shannon and surrounding countryside.
Castle Street, Limerick. Tel: 061– 411201/2. Open: daily 9.30am–5.30pm. Admission charge.

LOUGH GUR STONE AGE CENTRE

The area around Lough Gur is one of Ireland's most important archaeological sites, with numerous megalithic remains – stone circles, dolmens, wedge-shaped gallery graves and the sites of neolithic dwellings. A wealth of artefacts has been discovered in and around the lake. An audio-visual presentation of the Lough

Gur story is given in the 'neolithic-style' Stone Age Interpretative Centre.
Signposted 17km south of Limerick off the R512 to Kilmallock. Tel: 061–385186. Open: May to September, daily 10am–6pm. Admission charge.

Charming 15th-century carved choir stalls, St Mary's Cathedral

ST MARY'S CATHEDRAL

Built as a palace in the 12th century, the cathedral (Protestant) still shows original architectural features. Misericords in the choir stalls, dating from the 15th century, bear grotesque carvings.

During summer months St Mary's is the setting for a colourful *son et lumière* show highlighting dramatic moments in the city's history.
Bridge Street, Limerick. Tel: 061–310293. Freely accessible. Telephone for times of son et lumière shows. Admission charge.

CO CLARE
AILLWEE CAVE

Hollows scraped out on the floor of the huge cave provide evidence of early occupation by the brown bear, which once prowled in the area surrounding The Burren. The cave, one of the oldest in Ireland estimated at two million years old, has a river, a waterfall and 1km of well-lit passages. Entry is through an award-winning visitor centre built into the hillside.

3km south of Ballyvaughan (signposted). Tel: 065–7077036. Open: mid-March to early November, daily 10am–dusk. Last tour: July and August, 6.30pm; rest of year, 5.30pm. Admission charge.

BUNRATTY CASTLE AND FOLK PARK

A restored Norman-Irish keep built in 1277, the castle houses a fine collection of furniture and furnishings from the 14th to the 17th centuries. Medieval banquets are a twice-nightly feature throughout the year. The Folk Park, in the castle grounds, is a reconstructed 19th-century street, with craft shops, general stores and post office. Traditional crafts are seen in action, and country meals are served in a barn restaurant.

On the N18, 12km northwest of Limerick. Tel: 061–361511. Open: daily 9.30am–5pm (until 7pm June to August). Last admission to castle, 4.30pm. Admission charge.

CRAGGAUNOWEN HISTORICAL PROJECT

Many skills of the distant past have been revived in this progressive project in the grounds of a restored 16th-century castle. The most dramatic reconstruction is that of a *crannog*, a Bronze Age lake dwelling. The replica of St Brendan's 6th-century leather boat, in which Tim Severin crossed the Atlantic, is also on show.

Off the R469, 10km south of Quin. Tel: 061–367178. Open: May to September, daily 10am–6pm. Admission charge.

Bunratty Folk Park – a living museum of traditional village life

NORTHERN IRELAND
Enniskillen ■ Belfast
Sligo
Galway REPUBLIC
OF Dublin
Limerick IRELAND
Killarney Waterford
Cork

Cork City

Cork is built on an island embraced by two channels of the River Lee. The city's twisting, hilly streets and narrow lanes create traffic delays at times, so walking is the best way to get around. There is much to enjoy in a city which has retained some of the old ambience of a tall ships port. *Allow 1½ hours.*

Begin at St Patrick's Bridge. Proceed right along Lavitt's Quay. Opposite Opera House Bridge turn left into Emmet Place.

1 EMMET PLACE

The concrete drabness of Cork's Opera House may come as a disappointment, but the theatre offers a full programme of classical and popular opera, ballet and drama. The adjacent Crawford Municipal Art Gallery has an extensive collection of local landscapes from the 18th and 19th centuries. Exhibitions by contemporary Irish and international artists are also staged. *At the bottom of Emmet Place continue west along Paul Street.*

2 PAUL STREET

Pedestrianised Paul Street has brought new life to the city centre, with restaurants, boutiques, art and craft studios, and street entertainment in an attractive piazza. Traditional

Near by

7 City Hall

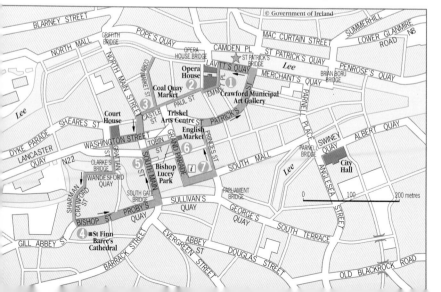

Cork – a delightful waterside city connected by bridges across the River Lee

Irish goods are available in the shops.
Continue west to the junction of Cornmarket Street and Castle Street.

3 CORNMARKET STREET
Coal Quay market stands at the junction and is the survivor of an open-air market that once continued along the length of Cornmarket Street. Today, the bulk of the area's trade is in second-hand clothing and antiques.
Follow Castle Street, turning left at North Main Street and right into Washington Street. At Grattan Street turn left, cross Clarke's Bridge and turn right on to Wandesford Quay, following Sharman Crawford Street to Bishop Street.

4 ST FINN BARRE'S CATHEDRAL
The cathedral's three spires give it a medieval look, but the building dates from the 19th century. Belonging to the Church of Ireland, it stands on the site of a monastery founded by St Finbarr in 650 (see page 71).
Follow Bishop Street to Proby's Quay, re-crossing the river at South Gate Bridge.

5 SOUTH MAIN STREET
South Main Street leads to two further centres of art and culture. Bishop Lucey Park, on the right, has a permanent exhibition of modern Cork sculpture. Also on the right, narrow Tobin Street leads to the Triskel Arts Centre, with exhibitions of contemporary arts and crafts, as well as film shows and stage productions.
Follow Tobin Street to Grand Parade.

6 GRAND PARADE
Spacious Grand Parade runs from crescent-shaped St Patrick's Street, Cork's main thoroughfare, to the south channel of the River Lee. About halfway along – close to where Tobin Street emerges – is the entrance to the English Market, a covered area of traditional stalls selling fish, meat, fruit and vegetables. At its southern end, the Parade has a monument to Irish patriots of the 18th and 19th centuries.
Turn left into South Mall.

7 SOUTH MALL
The start of South Mall is marked by a memorial to the Royal Munster Fusiliers who fell in World War I. Across the road, the roof of the Allied Irish Bank is supported by six marble pillars from Old St Paul's, London.
Turn left into Princes Street and right into St Patrick's Street, completing the walk at St Patrick's Bridge.

The Ring of Kerry

Justifiably the most popular excursion in Ireland, the 170km Ring of Kerry is a dramatic experience: a mix of rugged moorland and mountains, lakes, rivers and streams, cliffs, beaches and weatherbeaten islands. *Allow 1 day.*

Begin at the town of Killarney.

1 KILLARNEY

A comparatively modern resort – it sprang into prominence when 18th-century tourists were drawn to its wonderful setting – Killarney is a lively place where jaunting cars and coaches compete in busy streets. St Mary's Cathedral, completed in 1885, is the work of flamboyant architect Augustus Pugin. *Follow the N71 southwest for 18km to Ladies' View.*

Near by

1 Muckross Abbey and House (see page 73)

6 Darrynane House (see page 72)

2 LADIES' VIEW

The road soon weaves and climbs above the waters of Muckross Lake, and it is not difficult to understand the delight of Queen Victoria and her ladies-in-waiting, after whom the view is named. It is best seen from the second car park – a great panorama of the Killarney Valley.

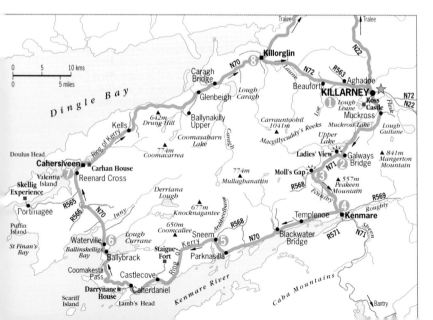

Continue along the N71 for 5km.

3 MOLL'S GAP

Another stunning viewpoint overlooks Macgillycuddy's Reeks and 1,041m-high Carrauntoohill, Ireland's highest mountain. The rounded rocks were formed by glacial action. Moll's Gap has a restaurant and craft shop.
Continue south for 10km to Kenmare.

4 KENMARE

The streets of Kenmare, reached after a drive across rugged mountain terrain, were laid out in an X-formation in 1775 by the first Marquess of Lansdowne. The town has an ancient stone circle, known locally as the Druid's Circle, on the banks of the River Finnihy.
Take the N70 west for 27km to Sneem.

5 SNEEM

The road follows the Kenmare River, and there are splendid views of the Caha and Slieve Miskish Mountains. Sneem, a pretty village with colourful houses surrounding a green, has good safe beaches. Fishing for salmon and brown trout is popular.

Four kilometres inland from Castlecove, on the N70, is Staigue Fort, about 2,500 years old and one of Ireland's best-preserved ancient structures.
Continue on the N70 for 35km to Waterville.

6 WATERVILLE

Waterville, best known today for its championship golf course and salmon fishing, is said to be the landing place of Noah's grandson Beith and granddaughter Cessair, who had failed to gain places on the Ark and had to build their own.

Jaunting car rides are a popular way to enjoy the delights of Killarney town

Drive north for 16km to Cahersiveen.

7 CAHERSIVEEN

South Kerry's major shopping town, Cahirsiveen is a place with strong associations with the patriot Daniel O'Connell. The Liberator's birthplace, ruined Carhan House, is 1.5km north of the town. The town is also the terminus for a ferry service to Valentia Island, which has nothing but 3,000km of ocean between it and Newfoundland (see also **Skellig Experience** page 74).
Follow the N70 for another 40km to Killorglin.

8 KILLORGLIN

The road skirts Dingle Bay, with views to the north of the Dingle Peninsula's peaks, and passes through the resort of Glenbeigh. Killorglin, a hillside town, is best known for its mid-August Puck Fair, a three-day festival based on the pagan custom of crowning a billy goat as King.
Take the N72 southeast for 21km to complete the drive at Killarney.

Connacht

Connacht, where Irish is a living language and University College Galway is a centre of Gaelic culture, has a range of beautiful scenery – from tranquil to wild and craggy. Its lakes and the shore of the River Shannon attract thousands of fishermen every year, and its extensive coastline caters for the sea angler, the yachtsman and the beach addict.

Lively Galway City combines a medieval atmosphere with a musical and cultural tradition which draws in young people from Europe and beyond each summer. Thousands more pour into Knock as pilgrims, worshipping in a church built in the 1970s to accommodate 20,000.

CO GALWAY

ALCOCK AND BROWN MEMORIAL

A cairn near the Marconi station ruins (see page 82) marks the place where intrepid aviators Alcock and Brown landed after the first non-stop transatlantic flight from St John's, Newfoundland, in 1919. On higher ground an aircraft monument marks the achievement.

Derrygimlagh Bog, 6km south of Clifden. Freely accessible.

ARAN ISLANDS

See pages 126–7.

AUGHNANURE CASTLE

Close to the shores of Lough Corrib, on rocky ground, this well-preserved 16th-century Irish tower house, built by the O'Flahertys, stands six storeys high. The remains of a banqueting hall, a circular watch-tower and a dry harbour can be seen.

Oughterard. Tel: 091–652214. Open: mid-June to mid-September, daily 9.30am–5.45pm. Admission charge.

CONNEMARA NATIONAL PARK

This 2,000-hectare area encompasses a range of habitats – heath, bogland, woodland and grassland – including four peaks of the Twelve Bens (Pins) mountain range. There are stunning views and a well-established herd of Connemara ponies roams the park.

The visitor centre provides detailed information on a variety of walks and nature trails.

Letterfrack, Connemara. Visitor Centre – tel: 095–41054. Open: May to September, daily 10am–6.30pm. Admission charge.

Ashleagh waterfall, near Leenane, in Connemara

COOLE NATURE RESERVE

The grounds of Lady Augusta Gregory's former estate, Coole Park, have become a nature reserve. This unique matrix of habitats incorporates a nature trail, a forest walk and a lake, and is home to a herd of red deer and other animal and bird species. There is an interpretative centre which explains the role of the reserve, as well as picnic sites and tea rooms. *Gort. Tel: 091–631804. Open: April to October, 9.30am–6.30pm (closes at 5pm and Mondays in spring). Admission charge.*

KYLEMORE ABBEY

This attractive lakeside abbey, originally built as a public residence, is now a convent for Benedictine nuns. Its Gothic chapel is a small-scale version of England's Norwich Cathedral. The 2.5ha Victorian walled garden, in its time one of the most impressive in Ireland, is currently under restoration. *18km from Clifden. Tel: 095–41146. Abbey: mid-March to November, 9.30am–6pm (4pm in winter). Grounds: Easter to October, noon–6pm. Admission charge.*

CONNACHT

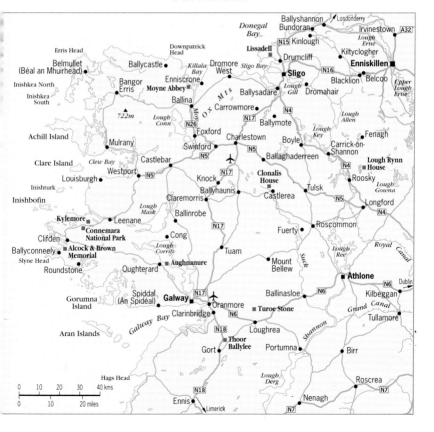

MARCONI WIRELESS STATION

Only the foundations and some of the masts remain of the first transatlantic wireless station, established by the Marconi company. The station was destroyed during fighting in the Irish Civil War (1922–3).

Derrygimlagh Bog, 6km south of Clifden. Freely accessible.

PORTUMNA WILDLIFE SANCTUARY

Portumna Forest Park, run by the Forest and Wildlife Service, has 400 hectares of walks in what was formerly the Harewood Estate. Bordered along its southern edges by Lough Derg, the sanctuary is home to a variety of animals, including red and fallow deer. A nature trail leaflet is available.

Near Portumna town, approaching from Woodford. Freely accessible.

SKY DRIVE

The Sky Drive, 14km of narrow road high over Clifden Bay, is one of the most scenic stretches of Co Galway, circling the peninsula west of the town and opening up vast seacapes. This road is very popular with landscape painters.

THOOR BALLYLEE

This former summer house of W B Yeats, where he wrote most of his works, has been restored to look as it did in his time. The 16th-century tower house contains a display of first editions of his work and visitors can 'climb the narrow, winding stair'. There is an audio-visual presentation of the poet's life, as well as a bookshop, craft shop, tea room, gardens and picnic area.

Gort. Tel: 091–631436. Open: Easter to September, daily 10am–6pm. Admission charge.

The Turoe Stone, enigmatic, but possibly a component in ancient fertility rites

TUROE STONE

Believed to date from the first century, this large granite boulder, standing in a field, is a rare example of a decorated Celtic pillar stone, with fine La Tène sculpting.

5km north of Loughrea, near Bullaun. Freely accessible.

CO MAYO

ACHILL ISLAND

Reached by a short causeway, Achill Island is the largest of Ireland's islands. Its economy depends largely on tourism as little of the island's 15,000 hectares can be cultivated – it is mostly mountain or bogland covered in heather. There are weird rock formations in the cliffs flanking the 3km beach at Keel, and the Atlantic Drive provides excellent views of the foothills and sandy beaches.

Boats can be hired at Keel Harbour for shark and other big-game fishing or to enjoy the dramatic cliff scenery. Stone circles and dolmens are dotted about inland.

Reached from Mulrany on the mainland.

ASHFORD CASTLE

Formerly a home of the Guinness family, this turreted castle, set on the shores of Lough Corrib, is now one of Ireland's most luxurious hotels. Its prestigious guest-list includes former US President, Ronald Reagan. The village of Cong was used as the location for the 1952 John Wayne film, *The Quiet Man*.
Cong. Tel: 092–46003. Hotel closed to non-residents. Grounds open: dawn to dusk. Admission charge.

CÉIDE FIELDS

An environmental interpretive centre, with audio-visual presentations, opened in 1992 at this extensive Stone-Age settlement, where tombs, 5,000-year-old dwellings, rare plants and rock formations can be seen.
8km west of Ballycastle. Tel: 096–43325. Open: mid-March to October, daily 10am–5pm (extended hours in summer). Guided tours of site. Admission charge.

CLARE ISLAND

See page 127.

CONG ABBEY

Completed in 1128 for the Augustinians, Cong Abbey replaced a former church built during the 6th or 7th century and destroyed by the Norsemen. It was founded by Turlough O'Connor, High King of Ireland, whose son, Roderick, destined to be the last High King, died in the abbey in 1198. The restored cloister and the monks' fishing house, built on a river platform, can still be seen. The abbey was an important ecclesiastical centre for more than 700 years, and some 3,000 people once lived there. The last Abbot of Cong died in 1829.
Cong, between Lough Mask and Lough Corrib. Freely accessible.

The excellent sandy beach on Achill, Ireland's largest island

FOXFORD WOOLLEN MILLS VISITORS CENTRE

The story of this 19th-century working mill, from the famine years to the present day, is told in an animated presentation. A tour of the mill shows Foxford tweeds, rugs and blankets being produced.
Foxford. Tel: 094–56756. Open: Monday to Saturday 10am–6pm, Sunday 2–6pm (tour every 20 minutes). Admission charge.

INISHKEA ISLANDS

These two low-lying, exposed islands form a sanctuary for up to 60 per cent of the Irish winter population of barnacle geese – some 2,900 birds. There are also early Christian remains connected with St Columba here.
4km west of Mullet Peninsula.

Many thousands visit Knock's shrine every year

KNOCK SHRINE

Pilgrims from around the world flock to Knock, where apparitions of the Virgin Mary were reported in 1879. Since then it has been regarded as the Lourdes of Ireland. A 20,000-seat circular church was built at the site in 1976 to accommodate the huge pilgrimages. Its finest hour came when Pope John Paul II visited the site in 1979.
On the N17, 15km south of Horan (Knock) International Airport. Tel: 094–88100. Freely accessible.

WESTPORT HOUSE

One of the most stately homes of Ireland, this handsome Georgian mansion, begun in 1730, was completed in 1788 for the Marquess of Sligo on the site of an earlier castle whose dungeons still exist. The architect was Richard Castle, whose work was re-modelled by James Wyatt. It is a place of contrasts – antique silver, Waterford glass, Georgian and Victorian furniture, and family portraits by Reynolds are on display, while video games flash in the dungeons. Ireland's premier family leisure park is set up in the small lakeside grounds, and includes a childrens zoo.
Near to The Quay, Westport. Tel: 098–25141. Open: June to September, Monday to Saturday 10.30am–6pm, Sunday 2–6pm. Admission charge.

WESTPORT TOWN

Westport town was designed by the architect James Wyatt and built on land owned by the Marquess of Sligo. With an octagonal centre, lime trees lining either side of a canalised river, Clew Bay at its feet and a wealth of grand Georgian buildings, the town attracts many visitors.

The Thursday morning market at the Octagon brings the farmers into town, and there is a frenzy of buying and selling at the clothes, produce and novelty stalls. It is even more lively when the annual Westport Arts Festival takes place from mid- to late September with events encompassing music, drama, film opera, art and free street entertainment.

CO SLIGO

CARROWMORE

The largest cemetery of megalithic tombs in Ireland can be seen at the top of a mountain at Carrowmore. More than 60 tombs, a variety of dolmens, passage graves and stone circles extend over half a square kilometre. One of the tombs dates back more than 6,000 years, while the Bronze-Age standing stones are thought to be from 1750BC. A visitor centre contains an exhibition about Stone-Age man and the excavations.

5km west of Sigo, east of Knocknarea Hill, on the R292. Freely accessible. Visitor Centre (tel: 071–615340) open: May to September, daily 9.30am–6.30pm.

CAVES OF KEASH

Seventeen small caves on the western side of a mountain show traces of human occupation, and the remains of cave bears, Arctic lemmings, Irish elk and reindeer were also discovered. According to legend, it was in one of these caves that Cormac MacAirt, King of Cashel, was reared by a she-wolf.

On the R295, 10km south of Ballymote. Freely accessible.

DRUMCLIFF MONASTIC SITE

Little is left of this 6th-century settlement except the stump of a round tower on one side of the N15 road and an elaborately carved 1,000-year-old high cross on the other. The carvings on the cross depict a selection of biblical scenes (see page 95).

7.5km north of Sligo. Freely accessible.

Westport has a rich legacy of fine town houses and spacious streets

COUNTRY LIFE

Rural life is *the* way of life to a large proportion of Irish people. Apart from the conurbations with six-figure populations – Dublin, Cork, Limerick and Belfast – towns are small islands of activity in a brilliant green landscape, where agriculture makes a vital contribution to the economy.

In the Republic some 5½ million of the country's 7 million hectares are devoted to agriculture, and about 14 per cent of the workforce is directly involved in it.

Farming, forestry and fishing are important industries in Northern Ireland. So it is no surprise that such events as show jumping, horse-racing, agricultural shows and ploughing matches attract huge numbers of spectators or that hunting, shooting and fishing are pursuits enjoyed by many thousands.

Small fields enclosed by low stone walls give way to open bogland, rich reddish-brown, or tiny rural main road villages. Barley, wheat, sugar beet and potatoes grow well in the rich, moist soil, but it is sheep and cattle rearing and dairy products that represent most of the agricultural output. Even on busy main roads motorists must be prepared to encounter a herd of cows or flock of sheep.

Living in isolated farms and cottages, the people are nevertheless gregarious, enjoying the social, sporting and cultural life to be found in bars and church halls, dance halls and playing fields.

On market days the country goes to town. Jam-packed at the bar after

Country life in Ireland
is closely linked to
agriculture – you can't
even escape it on the
roads

several hours of dealing, the farming
fraternity, exuding a heady smell of
damp tweed, presents a haze of flat
caps, gleaming gaiters, gnarled knowing
faces and sage comments.

HALF MOON BAY SCULPTURE TRAIL

A unique collection of wooden sculptures are dispersed throughout Hazelwood Forest, on the northern shore of Lough Gill. The sculptures range from figures from Irish legend to art nouveau forms by Irish and foreign sculptors, and can be seen by following forest trails starting at the car park.
Hazelwood Forest, 3km from Sligo, off the Dromahaire road. Freely accessible.

INNISCRONE (ENNISCRONE)

Seaweed found at this seaside resort, 53km west of Sligo, by Killala Bay, is renowned for its curative properties. People travel from far and wide to submerge themselves in the hot, seaweed-enriched salt water at the town's bath houses. Just north of the town is the Valley of Diamonds – a shell collector's paradise.

Kilcullen, Inniscrone. Bath House opening times vary: check tourist office for details (tel: 096–36202). Admission charge.

INNISFREE

There are daily boat trips from Sligo Town and Parkes Castle (see page 91) to this Lough Gill island, immortalised by the poet Yeats. But those content to look from a distance can see it from the shore.
Lough Gill, east of Sligo. Freely accessible. Boat trips: Wild Rose Water Bus (tel: 071–64266 for schedule).

LISSADELL HOUSE

Lissadell House is the home of the distinguished Gore-Booth family, two of whom – Eva and Constance – were friends of W B Yeats. He wrote a poem to them, *In Memory of Eva Gore-Booth and Con Markievicz* which is on display by the main gate. The contents of the house reflect the family's colourful lives.

Left: Lissadell – home of the Gore-Booths

Part of the estate is a forestry, wildlife and bird reserve, known locally as the 'Goose Field' because it has Ireland's largest colony of barnacle geese – immigrants from Greenland. The key to a bird hide, is available from the reserve warden. Seals can sometimes be seen on a sand-bank in the nearby bay.
Signposted from the N51 at Carney. Tel: 071–63150. Open: June to mid-September, Monday to Saturday 10.30am–12.30pm, 2–4.30pm. Admission charge.

STRANDHILL

Strandhill is a quiet seaside village with a good beach, and excellent facilities for surfing, but swimming is not safe.

Dolly's Cottage, a small folk museum housed in a 19th-century dwelling, sells home-made produce and sometimes holds evening traditional music sessions.
Strandhill, near Sligo Airport. Dolly's Cottage open: afternoons in summer. Free.

YEATS' GRAVE

Though he died in Roquebrune, France, W B Yeats was eventually buried at Drumcliff (see page 85). Tidily maintained, the plain grave of the poet lies within the shadow of the flat-topped Benbulben Mountain. The headstone bears an inscription from his final poem:
*Cast a cold Eye
On Life, on Death.
Horseman, pass by!*
The church houses a Visitors Centre outlining the history of the church and Drumcliff.
Drumcliff, 7.5km north of Sligo on the N15. Grave freely accessible. Visitors Centre (tel: 071–44956) open: Monday to Friday 8.30am–6pm, Saturday 10am–6pm, Sunday 1–6pm. Admission charge.

CO ROSCOMMON

BOYLE ABBEY

The impressive ruins of this Cistercian abbey show traces of their original splendour. The nave, with both Romanesque and Gothic arches, and the choir and transepts of the 12th-century church are still in good condition.
Boyle. Tel: 079–62604. Open: mid-June to mid-September, daily 9.30am–1.30pm, 2.30–6.30pm. Admission charge.

CLONALIS HOUSE

Clonalis is the ancestral home of the clan O'Conor, who claim to be Europe's oldest family, tracing their ancestry to AD75. The 19th-century mansion has items associated with the family, including the harp of Irish musician, Turlough O'Carolan (1630–1738).
Castlerea. Tel: 0907–20014. Open: June to mid-September, Tuesday to Sunday noon–5pm. Admission charge.

Castlerea is Co Roscommon's third largest town, and is known mainly as the birthplace, in 1815, of Sir William Wilde, the father of Oscar.

FUERTY

In the graveyard are the ruins of a Franciscan church in which 100 priests were killed by a local tyrant, Robert Ormsby, at the time of Cromwell's plundering. Carvings on the headstone of a blacksmith's grave show the tools of his trade – anvil, bellows and tongs, while a shepherd's headstone depicts sheep and a crook. The county's economy is still based on sheep and cattle, and Roscommon has one of Ireland's leading weekly livestock markets.
5km southwest of Roscommon.

ROSCOMMON

All the public hangings in County Roscommon took place at Roscommon Gaol. One of the inmates long ago, the notorious 'Lady Betty' was found guilty of the murder of her son, but had her death sentence commuted on condition that she carried out all further hangings without fee or reward. She accepted the deal, which is commemorated with a plaque. The 18th-century gaol fell into disuse in 1822. Part of the solid stone wall of the gaol has been incorporated into a development of shops.

Roscommon's Norman castle was built, captured by the Irish who razed it to the ground, and re-built all in the space of 11 years, from 1269 to 1280. Massive and roofless, though otherwise reasonably well preserved, it stands sombrely north of town.

Situated on the outskirts of Roscommon, on the road to Boyle, is the impressive ruin of Roscommon Abbey. This Dominican priory was founded in 1253 and somehow survived the religious persecution that followed the Reformation. Eight sculpted figures can be seen at the base of the tomb of Felim O'Conor, King of Connacht, in the remains of a substantial church. These sculpted figures depict gallowglasses – medieval Irish professional soldiers.

CO LEITRIM

Leitrim is Ireland's least populated county. Its largest town, Carrick-on-Shannon, has a population of fewer than 2,000. Anglers appreciate its many lakes and rivers, including a large section of the Shannon.

CO LEITRIM
FENAGH

It is believed that the small village of Fenagh was thickly populated in pre-Christian times because of the number of megalithic burial chambers.
Near Ballinamore.

GLENCAR WATERFALL

From the N16 Manorhamilton to Sligo road you will see the 17m-high waterfall tumbling in an unbroken leap into Glencar Lough long before the right turn that leads you to it. There are several waterfalls near by, but this is the highest. Yeats immortalised it in his poem *The Stolen Child*.
East of Drumcliff. Freely accessible.

Lough Key is the star attraction in the picturesque forest park

Sturdy Parke's Castle offers a superb view over the lovely Lough Gill

KILTYCLOGHER

Sean MacDiarmada, who was executed in Dublin for his part in the 1916 Easter Rising, was born here. The three-roomed thatched cottage where he once lived, now has almost national-shrine status. A statue of MacDiarmada stands in the village.

Take the Glenfarn road from Kiltyclogher; the house is 2km up a narrow road. For information tel: 71 61201. Open: during summer months only. Admission charge.

KINLOUGH FOLK MUSEUM

Kinlough's folk museum may be small, but it is crammed with fascinating items – documents, household and agricultural artefacts and a whiskey still.

Barrack Street, Kinlough. No telephone. Key from the grocer's shop opposite. Free.

LOUGH KEY FOREST PARK

Close to the county capital, Carrick-on-Shannon, this forest park lies along the banks of Lough Key. It has nature trails, bog gardens, a deer enclosure, boating facilities and a restaurant. Climb to the high ground, known as Moylurg Tower, for views of the surrounding countryside and the islands dotted across the lake.

East of Boyle on N4. Freely accessible. Charge for car park.

PARKE'S CASTLE

This strongly fortified 17th-century manor house was the home of an Englishman, Robert Parke, who undiplomatically dismantled a neighbouring castle to provide the material to build his own. The castle had been owned by the powerful O'Rourke clan, and as a result Parke's home needed to be impregnable as a defence against the outraged Irish. The last residing member of the O'Rourke clan harboured a Spanish Armada officer and was executed for treason. A video presentation relates the story, and there is a guided tour (see page 95).

North of Dromahair, on the north shore of Lough Gill. Tel: 071–64149. Open: St Patrick's weekend (nearest weekend to 17th March), April, May and October, daily 10am–5pm; June to September, daily 9.30am–6.30pm. Admission charge. Parkes Castle can be reached by boat from Sligo – Wild Rose Water Bus, tel: 071–64266 for time schedule.

Galway City

Prosperous, vibrant and compact, historic Galway is ideal for touring on foot. *Allow 1½ hours.*

Begin on the southeast side of Eyre Square, in front of the Galway Great Southern Hotel (the rail and bus stations are behind the hotel, on Station Road).

1 EYRE SQUARE

The square is surrounded by Galway's liveliest pubs and eating places. Its central area – Kennedy Park – is the setting for outdoor performances during the city's many festivals. The 6m steel sculpture, the work of Eamonn O'Donnel, symbolises the Galway 'hookers', traditional ships that once plied Galway Bay.

Near by

6 St Nicholas' Cathedral

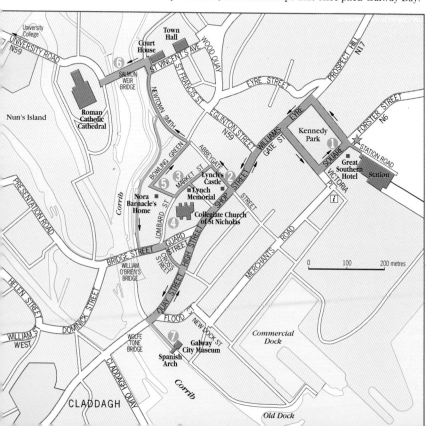

From the square's northwest corner follow Williamsgate Street to William Street and continue to Abbeygate Street.

2 LYNCH'S CASTLE
The Allied Irish Bank on the corner of Shop Street and Abbeygate Street is the best-preserved example of a merchant's town castle. Believed to have been built in the reign of Henry VIII, it features impressive coats-of-arms and fine fireplaces.
Turn right into Abbeygate Street and left into Market Street.

3 LYNCH MEMORIAL
An inscription on black marble set above a Gothic doorway marks the spot where, so local legend says, a 16th-century mayor of Galway found his own son guilty of murder, then hanged the boy himself when the executioner refused to carry out the sentence.
Continue to Lombard Street.

4 COLLEGIATE CHURCH OF ST NICHOLAS
Built by the Anglo-Normans in 1320 and enlarged in the 15th and 16th centuries, the church has many fine medieval carvings and relics and a peal of eight bells. A colourful street market spills around the church on Saturdays.
Take Bowling Green.

5 NORA BARNACLE'S HOME
A memorial plaque marks the former home of Nora Barnacle, James Joyce's wife. It was unveiled in 1982 to mark the centenary of his birth. The house is open to the public (Monday to Saturday, admission charge).
At the end of Bowling Green turn left into Newton Smith and continue to where Salmon Weir Bridge crosses the River Corrib.

Memorial to the plucky salmon

6 SALMON WEIR BRIDGE
Galway's best-known attraction, the bridge is the place from which shoals of salmon can be seen as they make their way upstream to spawn from mid-April to early July.
Follow the signed riverside walk to William O'Brien's Bridge, bear left along Bridge Street, right into Cross Street, and right into Quay Street to the Spanish Arch.

7 SPANISH ARCH
Built in 1594, the arch once protected the quays on which Spanish galleons unloaded. Today, it adjoins the Galway City Museum. Claddagh, viewed across the River Corrib, is the former fishing village where the traditional Irish wedding ring is said to have originated.
Return along Quay Street through the shopping area of High Street and Shop Street to complete the walk at Eyre Square.

Yeats' Country

The distinctive profile of Benbulben broods over Sligo Bay and appears unexpectedly, ever changing in the area's capricious climate. The drive embraces some of the places where the poet W B Yeats found inspiration. *Allow 1 day.*

Begin at Sligo Town.

1 SLIGO, CO SLIGO

Sligo has a long and often violent history. In the 9th century it was attacked by the Vikings, followed by Irish and Anglo-Norman raiders. Its population was reduced by a third during Ireland's great famine. The only remains of its early days are the ruins of the 13th-century Dominican Abbey in Abbey Street. Sligo Municipal Art Gallery has many paintings by W B Yeats' father, John, and his brother, Jack. W B himself (1865–1939) is commemorated in the Yeats Memorial

Near by

2 Lissadell House (see pages 88–9)

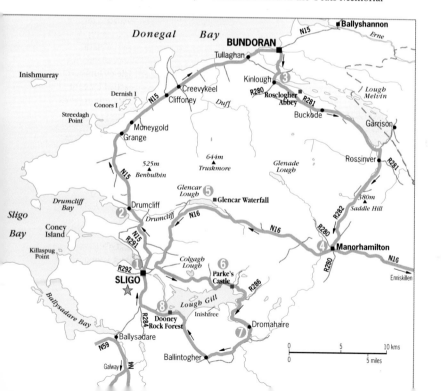

Building where the Yeats International Summer School is held each August. The Fiddler of Dooney competition, inspired by his poem, takes place at Sligo every July.
Take the N15 for 8km to Drumcliff.

2 DRUMCLIFF, CO SLIGO
The stump of a round tower and a thousand-year-old high cross are all that remain of a monastery thought to have been founded by St Columba in the 6th century (see page 85). Yeats' simple grave is to the left of the entrance to the grim Protestant church (see page 89).
Continue on the N15 for 37km to Bundoran, then take the R280 for 5km to Kinlough.

3 KINLOUGH, CO LEITRIM
An attractive village with excellent coarse and salmon fishing facilities, Kinlough overlooks Lough Melvin and the ruins of Rossclogher Abbey.
Take the R281 along the south shore of Lough Melvin for 13km. Turn right on to the R282 for 13km to Manorhamilton.

4 MANORHAMILTON, CO LEITRIM
This workaday community was named after a 17th-century Scottish 'planter', Sir Frederick Hamilton, who built the now ruined castle overlooking the town. A heritage centre (open May to September) tells the castle's history.
Follow the N16 west for about 13km to Glencar Lake.

5 GLENCAR, CO LEITRIM
The N16 skirts the lake, presenting wonderful alpine views of the Glencar Waterfall immortalised in the famous Yeats' poem, *The Stolen Child* (see page 90). The Glencar Valley is an ecological

pot-pourri, with mixed woodland and rare species of plant life.
Continue along the N16 for about 16km, then turn left to Parke's Castle on the R286.

Yeats, leader of the Irish literary revival and co-founder of Dublin's Abbey Theatre

6 PARKE'S CASTLE, CO LEITRIM
An impressively reconstructed manor house, Parke's Castle offers a superb view of Lough Gill, strewn with islands and surrounded by ancient woodland (see page 91). Yeats' Lake Isle of Innisfree (see page 88) can be reached by boat.
Continue on the R286, then turn right on the R288 for Dromahaire.

7 DROMAHAIRE, CO LEITRIM
Dromahaire hosts gatherings of the O'Rourke family. The village was laid out along the lines of a Somerset settlement by an English family, the Lane-Foxes.
Take the R287 followed by the R290 west to Dooney.

8 DOONEY, CO SLIGO
Dooney Rock Forest Park is in a lovely corner of Lough Gill. Here you will find the 'twining branches' mentioned in Yeats' poem *The Fiddler of Dooney*.
From Dooney take the N4 north to complete the drive at Sligo.

Ulster

*T*he ancient province of Ulster encompasses not only the six counties of Northern Ireland, but also Donegal, Cavan and Monaghan in the Republic. There is much to see – the incredibly beautiful Sperrin Mountains, the Antrim Coast Road and the glorious lakeland of Fermanagh, or travel across country to Londonderry and Donegal where beauty is revealed round every corner.

BELFAST
BELFAST ZOO
On the lower slopes of Cave Hill, over-looking the city, the zoo has a lake with flamingos, and a *crannog*, or fortified lake dwelling. There are red pandas, spectacled bears, rare tamarins and marmosets, sea lions and penguins.
Antrim Road, 6.5km north of Belfast. Tel: 028–9077 6277. Open: daily 10am–5pm (to 3.30pm, except Friday to 2.30pm, October to March). Admission charge.

BOTANIC GARDENS
Dominated by the elegant covered-glass and cast-iron Victorian Palm House, these pleasant gardens include a Tropical Ravine where many of the plants enclosed are over a century old.
Stranmillis Road, Belfast 7. Tel: 028–9032 4902. Open: daily dawn–dusk. Palm House and Tropical Ravine: Monday to Friday 10am–5pm, weekends and public holidays 2–5pm (to 4pm daily October to March); closed daily for lunch. Free.

CAVE HILL COUNTRY PARK
At the top of Cave Hill is MacArt's Fort, ancient earthworks where, in 1798, Wolfe Tone and United Irishmen colleagues asserted their independence from England. The impressive 19th-century Belfast Castle, contains a heritage centre.
6.5km north of Belfast. Tel: 028–9077 6925. Freely accessible. Heritage Centre open: daily 9am–6pm. Free.

CITY HALL

Just a village in the 17th century, by 1888 Belfast had nearly 300,000 people, and Queen Victoria gave it city status. Work began on the ornate City Hall, built in classical style with a high dome based on St Paul's Cathedral in London. It opened in 1906 (see page 116). *Donegall Square, Belfast 1. Tel: 028–9027 0456. Tours (advance bookings only): weekdays 10.30, 11.30am, 2.30pm, Saturday 2.30pm (2.30pm tours only in winter). Free.*

ULSTER

The unusual Sinclair Seamen's Church, with its unmistakable maritime atmosphere

CROWN LIQUOR SALOON

This ornately decorated, former railway hotel, with its gas lighting, fine wood panelling, highly decorated tiles and glass, is a popular rendezvous and one of Belfast's finest Victorian buildings (see page 117).
46 Great Victoria Street, Belfast 2. Tel: 028–9024 9476. Open: licensing hours.

GIANT'S RING

An intriguing circular megalithic enclosure nearly 200m in diameter, the ring has a central dolmen encircled by a high, thick bank of earth. The site, thought to be 4,000 years old, was used for horse-racing – three laps to the mile (1.6km) – in the 18th century.

Near Edenderry village, south Belfast, via Ballynahatty Road. Freely accessible.

GRAND OPERA HOUSE

Designed by the architect Frank Matcham and opened in 1895, this traditional Victorian theatre underwent substantial restoration and re-opened in 1980 (see page 117).
Great Victoria Street, Belfast 1. Tel: 028–9024 1919. Open: for performances.

LAGAN LOOKOUT CENTRE

Overlooking Belfast's River Lagan, the centre focuses on the city's social and industrial history.
Donegall Quay, Belfast 1. Tel: 028–9031 5444. Open: April to September, Monday to Friday 11am–5pm, Saturday and Sunday afternoons; October to March reduced hours and closed Monday. Admission charge.

QUEEN'S UNIVERSITY

The architectural style of the main building, designed by Sir Charles Lanyon, standing beyond a grassed area, with paved cloisters and a tower entrance, has echoes of Magdalen College at Oxford University in England. Other university buildings are dotted around Stranmillis Road. The Queen's Visitor Centre contains exhibitions and memorabilia.
University Road, Belfast 7. Visitor Centre – Tel: 028–9033 5252. Open: Monday to Friday 10am–4pm. Free.

ST ANNE'S CATHEDRAL

Building of this Anglican basilica in neo-Romanesque style began in 1899 and was completed 80 years later. Under the floor of the high nave lies the body of Lord Edward Carson, opposer of Home Rule.
Donegall Street, Belfast 1. Tel: 028–9032 8332. Guided tour: Monday to Saturday 10am–4pm. Donation appreciated.

SINCLAIR SEAMEN'S CHURCH

Sailors have worshipped here since 1853. Sermons are preached from a pulpit built like a ship's prow, and the organ has port and starboard navigation lights. *Corporation Square, Belfast 1. No telephone. Open: summer, Wednesday 2–4pm; services Sunday 11.30am and 7pm.*

STORMONT

The former Northern Ireland Parliament building is not open to the public, but people can wander in the parklands which line the 1.5km drive. *10km east of the city, off the Newtownards road, Belfast 9. Grounds are open during daylight hours. Free.*

BELFAST

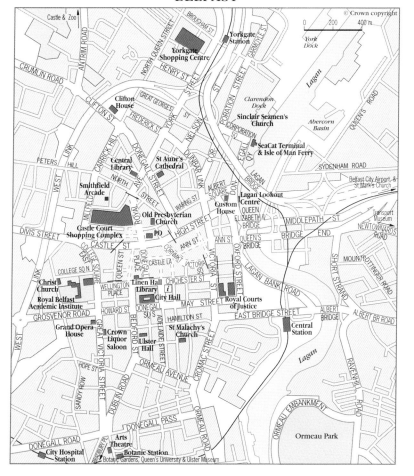
© Crown copyright

ULSTER MUSEUM

Gold and silver jewellery from the *Girona*, a Spanish Armada vessel wrecked off the Giant's Causeway in 1588, can be seen among exhibits covering 9,000 years. International art, Irish furniture, glass, and countless items of interest are on display. The museum has become an important world centre for Spanish Armada studies.

Botanic Gardens, Stranmillis Road, Belfast 7. Tel: 028–9038 3000. Open: Monday to Friday 10am–5pm, Saturday 1–5pm, Sunday 2–5pm. Free.

CO DOWN
ANNALONG CORN MILL

This early 19th-century water-powered mill, now restored to working order, has an exhibition explaining the history of flour milling. There is also a herb garden, a visitor centre, café and antiques shop.

Marine Park, Annalong. Tel: 028–4376 8736. Open: February to November, Tuesday to Saturday and public holidays 11am–5pm. Admission charge.

ARK OPEN FARM

Nigerian pygmy goats, miniature horses, Jacob's sheep, rare breeds of pig and other creatures are featured at this small farm, along with a pets' corner and pony rides.

296 Bangor Road, Newtownards. Tel: 028–9182 0445. Open: Monday to Saturday 10am–6pm, Sunday 2–6pm. Admission charge.

BALLYCOPELAND WINDMILL

This late 18th-century tower mill, which operated until 1915, is once again working. There is an electrically-run model of the mill, and a visitor centre in the miller's house.

On the B172, 1.5km west of Millisle. Tel: 028–9186 1413. Open: April to September, Tuesday to Saturday 10am–7pm, Sunday 2–7pm. Admission charge.

BRONTË HOMELAND INTERPRETIVE CENTRE

Drumballyroney school and church is where Patrick Brontë, father of the three literary sisters, taught and preached before moving to Yorkshire. Now preserved, the centre marks the start of a

One of several buildings reconstructed at the Ulster Folk and Transport Museum (see page 103)

Annalong's 19th-century cornmill stands on the edge of the harbour

13km scenic drive signposted 'Brontë Homeland', including Patrick's birthplace at Emdale.
Off the B10, 14km southeast of Banbridge. Tel: 028–4063 1152. Open: March to September, Tuesday to Friday 11am–5pm, weekends and public holidays 2–6pm. Admission charge.

CASTLE WARD

Very much a His and Hers house. He (Lord Bangor) wanted a classical Palladian home. She (his wife, Anne) wanted Strawberry Hill Gothic, which was all the rage in the 1760s. As a result, the front is classic, the back anything but. The marriage did not last, but the house, now a National Trust property, survives. Buildings include a cornmill, a sawmill, a dairy and a Victorian laundry. There is also a Victorian Pastimes Centre.
2.5km west of Strangford. Tel: 028–4488 1204. House open: June to September, Friday to Wednesday 1–6pm; spring and autumn weekends only. Estate: daylight hours year-round. Admission charge.

DOWN COUNTY MUSEUM

Housed in a former jail built in the late 18th century, this museum includes the St Patrick Heritage Centre, telling the story of the saint, plus local Stone-Age artefacts and Bronze-Age gold pieces.

The Mall, English Street, Downpatrick. Tel: 028–4461 5218. Open: Monday to Friday 11am–5pm, weekends 2–5pm. (closed Sunday and Monday in winter). Free.

DOWNPATRICK–ARDGLASS RAILWAY MUSEUM

A restored 1km section of the BCDR Downpatrick-Ardglass branch line runs from Market Street, Downpatrick. The steam engine *Guinness*, or one of two diesel locomotives, hauls the train on summer Sundays. There are also tours of the restored station and workshops.
Market Street, Downpatrick. Tel: 028–4461 5779. Open: July and August, Sunday and public holidays 2–5pm. Admission charge.

EXPLORIS

Many of the creatures that thrive in the waters of Strangford Lough (see page 103) can be viewed – and some touched –in this sea aquarium. The Lough's inhabitants include wolf fish and sharks.
The Rope Walk, Castle Street, Portaferry. Tel: 028–4272 8062. Open Monday to Friday 10am–6pm, Saturday 11am–6pm, Sunday 1–6pm (to 5pm in winter). Admission charge.

HILLSBOROUGH FORT

Built in 1650, Hillsborough Fort was re-modelled in the 18th century. Across the road is Hillsborough Castle which was the scene of the signing of the Anglo-Irish agreement in 1985, and is the former residence of the Governor of Northern Ireland.
Hillsborough. Tel: 028–9268 3285. Fort open: April to September, Tuesday to Saturday 10am–7pm, Sunday 2–7pm (to 4pm in winter); grounds open until dusk. Free.

INCH ABBEY

This ruined Cistercian abbey, in a lovely woodland setting in the Quoile marshes, is approached by a causeway. John de Courcey founded the abbey in the 1180s on the site of a 9th-century monastery. The monks at Inch were English, having come from Furness Abbey, Lancashire. The triple east window still stands.
3km north of Downpatrick, off the A7.
Tel: 028–9023 5000 (Historic Monuments).
Open: April to September, Tuesday to Saturday 10am–7pm, Sunday 2–4pm; October to March, Saturday 10am–4pm, Sunday 2–4pm. Admission charge.

MOUNT STEWART

The magnificent gardens, created by Lady Londonderry in the 1920s, support an enormous plant collection which enjoys the mild climate. Each garden has a theme – the Italian garden, the Spanish garden, the Shamrock garden, the Peace garden. The house (National Trust) contains antique furniture from Europe, collections of

porcelain and important paintings. The Temple of the Winds is an 18th-century folly in classical Greek style, with views over Strangford Lough.
A20, 8km southeast of Newtownards. Tel: 028–4278 8387/8487. House open: Easter, May to September, Wednesday to Monday, 1–6pm; April and October weekend afternoons. Garden: March, Sunday 2–5pm; April to September, daily 11am–6pm; October, weekends 11am–6pm. Temple of the Winds: April to October, weekends 2–5pm. Admission charge.

ST PATRICK'S GRAVE

St Patrick is reputed to be buried near the site of an old round tower in the churchyard at Down Cathedral, along with the bones of St Brigid and St Columba. A granite slab covers the hole made by pilgrims' feet.
Downpatrick. Freely accessible.

SAUL

St Patrick is thought to have landed near Saul and founded his first church here. From here he travelled the country converting the Irish. The 1932 St Patrick's Memorial Church was built where St Patrick's Abbey is believed to have stood.
3km northeast of Downpatrick. Tel: 028–4461 4922. Open: daily.

SCRABO COUNTRY PARK

Built in 1857 as a memorial to the 3rd Marquis of Londonderry, Scrabo Tower now serves as a countryside centre with woodland walks, quarries and interesting wildlife. Visitors can climb the 122 steps to the top of the 41m-high tower for outstanding views over Strangford.
203a Scrabo Road, Newtownards. Tel: 028–9181 1491. Tower open: Easter, summer and public holidays. Phone for opening times. Free. Park: freely accessible.

Tribute at the grave of Ireland's patron saint

Mount Stewart's Italianate-style garden is one of the most outstanding in Ireland

STRANGFORD LOUGH
One of Europe's richest places for marine wildlife, this large sea inlet, studded with 120 islands, is home to hundreds of marine animal species – from molluscs and sponges to birds and large colonies of seals.

STRUELL WELLS
Four wells reputed to have healing powers, and first recorded in 1306, are fed by an underground stream. There are men's and women's bath houses and a drinking well built around 1600. Mass is celebrated at the site at midsummer.
Off the B1, 2.5km east of Downpatrick. Tel: 028–9023 5000 (Historic Monuments). Freely accessible.

ULSTER FOLK AND TRANSPORT MUSEUM
Original farmhouses, cottages, watermills, a church, a school and village buildings were moved stone by stone and re-erected to form this highly acclaimed outdoor museum. Inside, the transport section ranges from donkey creels to aircraft.
Cultra, Holywood, 11km east of Belfast. Tel: 028–9042 8428. Open: April to September, Monday to Friday 9.30am–5pm (10.30am–6pm July and August), Saturday 10.30am–6pm, Sunday noon–6pm (reduced hours in winter). Admission charge.

CO ARMAGH
ARDRESS HOUSE
This 17th-century farmhouse has a fine 18th-century front and an elegant drawing room with superb neo-classical plasterwork. The grounds contain a cobbled farmyard with livestock, and a woodland walk – the Ladies' Mile – surrounds the estate.
On the B28 at Annaghmore, 11km west of Portadown. Tel: 028–3885 1236. Open: Easter, April and September, weekends and public holidays 2–6pm; July and August, Wednesday to Monday noon–6pm. Admission charge.

RELIGION

There are few countries in the western world where religion is so much a part of the everyday scene. The differences between the two Irelands are characterised by the number of Marian grottoes and shrines (Roman Catholic) in the Republic and the dour chapels and Orange Order halls (Protestant) in the North.

All over the island there are hundreds of ruined churches, many of them still playing an important role.

On both sides of the border, churches built since the 19th century tend to be stark: gaunt, steepled buildings pointing a granite-grey finger at the sky. But their huge car parks testify to the size of church-going communities.

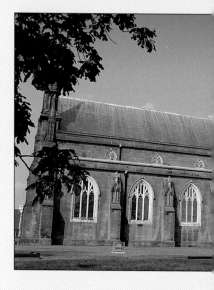

Above: St Patrick's Church of Ireland Cathedral, Armagh
Below: a wayside shrine in honour of the Blessed Virgin Mary
Below left: march of the Orange Order

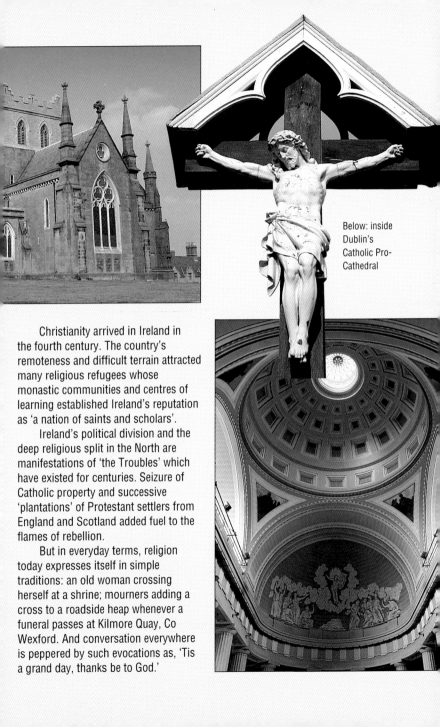

Below: inside Dublin's Catholic Pro-Cathedral

Christianity arrived in Ireland in the fourth century. The country's remoteness and difficult terrain attracted many religious refugees whose monastic communities and centres of learning established Ireland's reputation as 'a nation of saints and scholars'.

Ireland's political division and the deep religious split in the North are manifestations of 'the Troubles' which have existed for centuries. Seizure of Catholic property and successive 'plantations' of Protestant settlers from England and Scotland added fuel to the flames of rebellion.

But in everyday terms, religion today expresses itself in simple traditions: an old woman crossing herself at a shrine; mourners adding a cross to a roadside heap whenever a funeral passes at Kilmore Quay, Co Wexford. And conversation everywhere is peppered by such evocations as, 'Tis a grand day, thanks be to God.'

THE ARGORY

The Argory is a neo-classical 1820s
mansion with an imposing stable yard
and sundial garden in 121 hectares of
wooded countryside overlooking the
River Blackwater. The house contains a
collection of antique furniture and an
acetylene gas plant which still lights
some of the rooms.

*Derrycaw Road, 6.5km northeast of Moy.
Tel: 028–8778 4753. Open: Easter 2–6pm;
April to June and September, weekends
2–6pm; July and August, Wednesday to
Monday 2–6pm. Public holidays from 1pm.
Admission charge.*

ARMAGH FRIARY

Set in the grounds of the Archbishop's
Palace are the ruins of the longest friary
in Ireland, founded for the Franciscans in
1263 by Archbishop Patrick O'Scanail.
The **Palace Stables Heritage Centre**
portrays typical daily life in the
Archbishop's Palace in 1776. There are
working stables, a smithy, craft
demonstrations and exhibitions.

*Friary Road, Armagh. Tel: 028–3752
9629. Friary: freely accessible. Heritage
Centre: April to August, Monday to
Saturday 10am–5.30pm, Sunday 1–6pm
(reduced hours in winter). Admission
charge.*

ARMAGH PLANETARIUM

Visitors can experience space travel
through the latest hands-on computer
exhibits in the planetarium's Hall of
Astronomy. The planetarium theatre has
a worldwide reputation for its innovative
'star shows' (booking advised). On
display are astronomical instruments.

*College Hill, Armagh. Tel: 028–3752
3689. Open: Monday to Friday
10am–4.45pm, weekends 1.15–4.45pm.
Shows every afternoon. Admission charge.*

The Sundial Garden at The Argory

GOSFORD FOREST PARK

Several of the walks through the former
demesne of Gosford Castle, in early
19th-century mock-Norman style, were
devised by Jonathan Swift, author of
Gulliver's Travels. Traditional breeds of
poultry strut in open paddocks, and
ornamental pigeons coo in a dovecote.
The estate also includes a deer park,
walled garden and nature trail.

*Gosford Road, Markethill. Tel: 028–3755
1277. Castle: not open to the public.
Park open: daily 10am–dusk. Admission
charge.*

KILLEVY CHURCHES

Joined together by a common gable,
these two churches, one 11th-century,
the other 13th-century, are on the site of
a nunnery which survived from the 5th
century until the Dissolution in 1542.
Its founder, St Monenna (also known as
St Bline) is believed to be buried under
a granite slab in the graveyard.

*Signposted off the B113, 6km southwest of
Newry. Freely accessible.*

LOUGH NEAGH DISCOVERY
CENTRE

This centre on Oxford Island has a
wildlife exhibition and there are boat
trips, and talks on the flora and fauna of
the Lough Neagh basin. Oxford Island

is a birdwatcher's paradise with more than 8km of walks and viewing hides.
Oxford Island, exit 10 from the M1. Tel: 028–3832 2205. Open: April to September, daily 10am–7pm; October to March, Wednesday to Sunday 10am–5pm. Admission charge.

NAVAN CENTRE

The history and legends of the great Iron Age hill fort, which was once the ancient capital of the Kings of Ulster, are told here with the aid of computer technology.
On the A28, 1.5km west of Armagh. Tel: 028–3752 5550. Open: Fort – freely accessible. Visitor Centre – April to June and September, Monday to Saturday 10am–6pm, Sunday 11am–6pm; July and August, Monday to Saturday 10am–7pm, Sunday 11am–7pm; October to March, Monday to Friday 10am–5pm, Saturday 11am–5pm, Sunday noon–5pm. Admission charge.

Computerised exhibits at Armagh's Planetarium

PEATLANDS PARK

This park tells the story of peat boglands over a period of 10,000 years. There are areas of cutaway bogland, virgin bogs, small lakes and low wooded hills. A narrow-gauge railway, originally used for carrying turf, takes visitors out on to the bog to prevent erosion.
Exit 13 from the M1, 11km east of Dungannon, Co Tyrone. Tel: 028–3885 1102. Open: daily 9am–dusk. Visitor Centre – Easter to May and September, weekends and public holidays 2–6pm; June to August, daily 2–6pm. Charge for railway.

ROYAL IRISH FUSILIERS MUSEUM

This museum relates the regiment's history from 1793 to 1968. Exhibits include a soldier's uniform from the Peninsular War and a 1943 Christmas card from Adolf Hitler.
Sovereigns House, Mall East, Armagh. Tel: 028–3752 2911. Open: Monday to Friday 10am–12.30pm, 1.30–4pm (Saturdays also in summer). Admission charge.

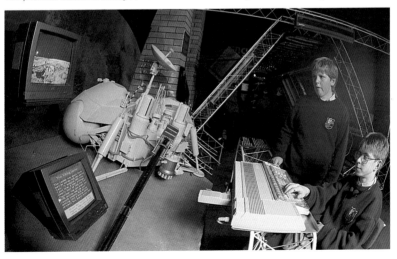

ST PATRICK'S TRIAN

Three attractions in one are presented at this interpretive centre. The 'Armagh Story' traces developments from prehistoric times to the present day. 'The Least of All The Faithful' features St Patrick, who built a church here in the 5th century. The other attraction, of particular interest to children, celebrates 'The Land of Lilliput', based on Dean Swift's *Gulliver's Travels*. There is also a restaurant.
40 English Street, Armagh. Tel: 028–3752 1801. Open: July and August, Monday to Saturday 10am–5.30pm, Sunday 1–6pm; September to June, Monday to Saturday 10am–5pm, Sunday 2–5pm. Admission charge.

CO MONAGHAN
COUNTY MUSEUM

Monaghan's county museum, housed in an 18th-century market house in the country town, is an award-winning museum with exhibits representing 200 years of local history, while pride of place goes to the 600-year-old bronze processional Cross of Clogher.
Hill Street, Monaghan. Tel: 047–82928. Open: Tuesday to Saturday 11am–5pm. Closed: October to May from 1–2pm. Free.

CO CAVAN
CARRAIG CRAFT VISITORS CENTRE

Rod and rush basketwork in the form of hats, creels, bread baskets, shopping baskets and other items are displayed. The basketry museum has an audio-visual presentation and there are demonstrations, lectures and craft workshops.
Mount Nugent. Tel: 049–40179. Open: Monday to Saturday 10am–6pm, Sunday 2–6pm. Admission charge.

CAVAN COUNTY MUSEUM

The former convent of the Sisters of Poor Clare, this interesting museum traces the history of the county from pre-Christian times to the present day.
Virginia Road, Ballyjamesduff. Tel: 049–44070. Open: Tuesday to Saturday 10am–5pm. Free (charge for exhibitions).

CO FERMANAGH
BELLEEK POTTERY

Ireland's oldest pottery reveals the skills that produce its fine china and distinctive basketware. There are factory tours and visitors can take their time browsing in the museum, visitors' centre

Belleek is famed for its parian china

The Georgian splendour of Florence Court, in the grounds of its beautiful estate (see page 110)

and shop. The restaurant serves refreshment on fine Belleek tableware (see page 121).
Belleek. Tel: 028–6865 8501. Visitor centre open: March to September, Monday to Friday 9am–6pm, Saturday 10am–6pm, Sunday 2–6pm (to 8pm in July and August); October to February, Monday to Friday 9am–5.30pm, Saturday 10am–6pm, Sunday 11am–8pm. Tours: Monday to Thursday 9.30am–4.15pm, Friday 9.30am–3.15pm. Tour charge.

CASTLE ARCHDALE COUNTRY PARK

On the shores of Lower Lough Erne, the park has something for everyone – picnic areas, walks, open-air exhibits of natural history and agricultural machinery and an exhibition featuring the Battle of the Atlantic during World War II. Pony trekking, boat rental and cycle hire are available. There is a ruined castle in the surrounding woodlands and the marina has concrete jetties and slipways built for wartime flying boats (see page 121).
Off the B82, 5km south of Kesh. Tel: 028–6862 1588. Freely accessible.

CASTLE COOLE

The stateliest of the National Trust's stately homes in Northern Ireland, Castle Coole was completed in 1798. It was designed by James Wyatt and built for the Earls of Belmore. The house has an imposing Palladian front and there are fine furnishings and plasterwork within.
On the A4, 2.5km southeast of Enniskillen. Tel: 028–6632 2690. House open: Easter, April and September, weekends 1–6pm; May to August, Friday to Wednesday 1–6pm. Grounds open: dawn to dusk. Admission charge (grounds free in winter).

DEVENISH ISLAND

The island has extensive monastic ruins and probably Ireland's most perfect round tower. The earliest ruins and the tower are 12th-century, but the monastery was founded by St Molaise, (died 563), and remained an important religious centre until the 17th century.
By ferry from Trory Point, 5km north of Enniskillen, junction of the A32 and B82. Ferry departs Tuesday to Saturday 10am, 1, 3 and 5pm, Sunday 2, 3 and 4pm. Fare includes admission to tower and museum.

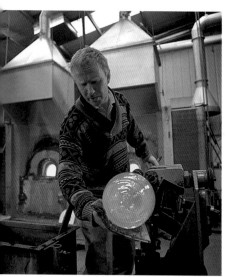

Glass maker at Tyrone Crystal, famous for its fine cut glass

FLORENCE COURT

One of Ulster's most important 18th-century houses, Florence Court was built by the Earls of Enniskillen. The house is noted for its extravagant rococo plasterwork and fine furniture. The surrounding forest park contains an ancient Irish yew tree, said to be the mother of all Irish yews (see page 121). *12km southwest of Enniskillen via the A4 and A32. Tel: 028–6634 8249. House open: Easter, April, May and September, week-ends 1–6pm (some afternoons also in summer). Grounds open: daily 10am–4pm. Admission charge (grounds free in winter).*

LOUGH NAVAR FOREST

Red deer and wild goats roam the forest, and a steep zigzag path, part of the Ulster Way, leads to one of the best panoramas in Ireland, with views across Lough Erne and to counties Donegal and Sligo.

Signposted off the A46, 8km northwest of Derrygonnelly. Tel: 028–6864 1256. Open: daily 10am–dusk. Admission charge.

MARBLE ARCH CAVES

One of Europe's finest cave systems can be toured by electric boat and on foot in a 75-minute guided exploration of underground rivers, waterfalls, winding passages and huge chambers with impressive stalagmite and stalactite formations. Over 300 million years of history is here in among a strange landscape of chasms and valleys. Take comfortable shoes and a sweater as it can get quite chilly. The visitor centre has an exhibition area, an audio-visual theatre and restaurant (see page 121). *19km southwest of Enniskillen, following the A4 (Sligo road) and the A32, near Florence Court. Tel: 028–6634 8855. Open: mid-March to September, daily 10am–5pm (weather permitting). Admission charge.*

REGIMENTAL MUSEUM OF THE ROYAL INNISKILLING FUSILIERS

Brightly coloured uniforms, arms and colours outline the story of this famous regiment, housed in the medieval castle of Enniskillen, seat of the Maguires. Exhibits include Napoleonic battle trophies, badges and medals, musical instruments and the bugle that sounded the charge at the Battle of the Somme in 1916 (see page 120). Also housed in the castle is the **Fermanagh County Museum**, with displays on the landscape and people of Fermanagh. *Castle Keep, Castle Barracks, Enniskillen. Tel: 028–6632 5000. Open: Tuesday to Friday 10am–5pm, Saturday and Monday 2–5pm, Sunday (July and August) 2–5pm. Closed weekends and Monday mornings, October to April. Admission charge.*

CO TYRONE

ALTMORE OPEN FARM

Visitors can learn the history of the Sperrin Mountains regions and see rare breeds of farm animals and poultry on this 71-hectare sheep farm. There is pony trekking in summer, and fishing.
32 Altmore Road, 5km south of Pomeroy. Tel: 028–8775 8977. Open: daily 9am–dusk. Admission charge.

ARDBOE CROSS

On the west shore of Lough Neagh is one of Ireland's finest northern high crosses, marking the site of a monastery. Over 5m high, this 10th-century cross has Old and New Testament scenes carved into it.
Lough Neagh, 16km east of Cookstown, off the B73. Freely accessible.

BEAGHMORE STONE CIRCLES

Beaghmore is a remarkable prehistoric site, unlike any other in Ireland. Consisting of seven Bronze Age stone circles in a complex ceremonial area, discovered beneath a layer of peat, its origins and purpose are unknown.
Signposted from the A505 between Cookstown and Gortin. Freely accessible.

PRESIDENT GRANT'S ANCESTRAL HOMESTEAD

John Simpson, great-grandfather of Ulysses S Grant, 18th President of the United States, was born at Ballygawley in 1738 and emigrated to Pennsylvania in 1760. The two-room thatched farmhouse where he lived has been restored, and the adjoining visitor centre has an audio-visual theatre and exhibits of rural life.
Dergina, Ballygawley. Tel: 028–8555 7133. Open: Easter to September, Monday to Saturday noon–5pm, Sunday 2–6pm. Admission charge.

TYRONE CRYSTAL

Visitors can tour the factory and watch the various stages – blowing, marking, cutting and finishing – in the production of fine glassware.
Killybrackey, Dungannon. Tel: 028–8772 5335. Tours: Monday to Thursday 9.30am–3.30pm, Friday 9.30am–noon (Saturday 9.30am–3.30pm in summer). Craft shop open: Monday to Saturday 9am–5pm. Admission charge.

ULSTER-AMERICAN FOLK PARK

This open-air museum traces the connections of famous Americans with their Ulster ancestry, from Davy Crockett to an Archbishop of New York, including a handful of US Presidents. The hard facts of 19th-century emigration are graphically demonstrated in the Ship and Dockside Gallery, where the smells and sounds of an overcrowded emigrant ship are reproduced.
Mellon Road, Castletown, 5km north of Omagh, on the A5. Tel: 028–8224 3292. Open: Easter to September, Monday to Saturday 11am– 6.30pm, Sunday and public holidays 11.30am–7pm (reduced hours in winter). Last admission 90 minutes before closing. Admission charge.

ULSTER HISTORY PARK

The human history of Ulster, from the arrival of primitive settlers in 8000BC to the end of the 17th century is presented, with reconstructions of Stone Age houses and round towers.
Cullion, 11km north of Omagh, on the B48. Tel: 028–8164 8188. Open: April to September, Monday to Saturday 10.30am– 6.30pm, Sunday 11.30am–7pm, public holidays 10.30am–7pm (reduced hours in winter). Last admission 90 minutes before closing. Admission charge.

WELLBROOK BEETLING MILL

An 18th-century water-powered mill, restored to working order by the National Trust, demonstrates beetling – the final process in which linen is hammered to give it its characteristic sheen.

Corkhill, Off the A505, 6.5km west of Cookstown. Tel: 028–8675 1735. Open: April to June and September, weekends and public holidays 2–6pm (weekday afternoons also in summer). Admission charge.

WILSON ANCESTRAL HOME

This simple thatched, whitewashed house in the Sperrin Mountains was the home of the grandfather of the 28th US President, Woodrow Wilson. It still contains some original furniture.

Dergalt, 3km southeast of Strabane. Tel: 028–7188 3735 for details. Admission charge.

Traditional methods are still used to produce fine pottery in Donegal

CO DONEGAL
DONEGAL CASTLE

Close to the town centre, this fortified manor house dates from the 15th century, but underwent much re-building in the early 17th century, when it was incorporated into a Jacobean structure by Sir Basil Brooke.

Tirchonaill Street, Donegal. Tel: 073–22405. Open: March to October, daily 9.30am–5.45pm. Admission charge.

DONEGAL COUNTY MUSEUM

Artefacts dating from the Stone Age to the Donegal Railway era are exhibited.

High Road, Letterkenny. Tel: 074–24613. Open: Monday to Friday 10am–4.30pm, Saturday 1–4.30pm. Free.

DONEGAL PARIAN CHINA

Short 15-minute tours of the factory give visitors an insight into the traditional methods used to produce this delicate china and porcelain. Products can be bought at factory prices. The guided tours run from Monday to Friday.

Ballyshannon. Tel: 072–51826. Open: March to September, Monday to Saturday 9am–5.30pm, Sunday 10.30am–4.30pm; October to December, Monday to Friday 9am–5.30pm. Free.

ERRIGAL MOUNTAIN

Errigal is Donegal's highest peak at 752m. Those who know say it is an easy climb; others say scrabbling on the loose scree and the near-perpendicular topmost peak can be daunting. All agree that the view from the summit is supreme.

Dunlewey, Freely accessible.

GLEBE GALLERY

The Glebe Gallery houses the art collection of Derek Hill, landscape and portrait painter, who worked here until

Glebe House contains Derek Hill's extensive art collection, which he presented to the nation

1954. He presented the house and collection, which includes works by Picasso and Renoir, to the nation in 1981.
On the shores of Garton Lough, by Glenveagh Park. Tel: 074–37071. Open: Easter week and mid-May to September, Saturday to Thursday 11am–6.30pm. Admission charge.

GLENCOLUMBKILLE FOLK VILLAGE MUSEUM

The Folk Village features a group of three traditional-style cottages spanning three centuries, each furnished according to the period it represents (1700s, 1800s and 1900s).
Glencolumbkille. Tel: 073–30017. Open: Easter to September, Monday to Saturday 10am–6pm, Sunday noon–6pm. Admission charge.

GLENVEAGH NATIONAL PARK AND CASTLE

Glenveagh is one of the last places in Ireland to be influenced by man. The Visitors Centre introduces the 16,000-hectare park's natural history – mountain moorland, lakes and woodland. The dramatically-sited castle here is set in glorious gardens. There are nature trails, and one of Ireland's last two herds of red deer live in the park.
Church Hill, 16km west of Letterkenny. Tel: 074–37008. Castle open: Easter to first Sunday in November, daily 10am–6.30pm (closed Friday in October and November). Tours. Admission charge to castle and park.

IONAD COIS LOCHA

Carding, spinning and weaving demonstrations, story-telling, boat trips, an adventure play area, farm tours and a craft shop feature in this award-winning lakeside centre where Irish is spoken.
Dunlewey, Letterkenny. Tel: 075–31699. Open: mid-March to early April, Saturday 10.30am–6pm, Sunday 11am–7pm; early April to early November, Monday to Saturday 10.30am–6pm, Sunday 11am–7pm. Admission charge.

TULLYARVAN MILL CULTURAL AND EXHIBITION CENTRE

Converted from a 19th-century corn mill, this visitor centre has a textile museum, wildlife display, art workshop, craft shop and coffee shop.
Buncrana, Inishowen. Tel: 077–61613. Open: June to September, Monday to Saturday 10am–6pm, Sunday 2–6pm. Admission charge.

CO LONDONDERRY
FOYLE VALLEY RAILWAY CENTRE

The centre outlines the region's railway history, featuring the narrow-gauge systems of the Co Donegal Railway and Londonderry & Lough Swilly Railway.
Foyle Road, Derry. Tel: 028–7126 5234. Open: April to September, Tuesday to Saturday 10am–4.30pm. Train rides at 2.30pm. Museum free; charge for train rides.

ROE VALLEY COUNTRY PARK

Ulster's first domestic hydroelectric power station, opened in 1896, is on show here, and much of its original equipment is preserved, together with old water mills for linen production.
Off the B192, 1.5km south of Limavady. Tel: 028–7772 2074. Open: visitor centre – daily 10am–5pm (to 4pm October to Easter). Free. Park freely accessible.

ST COLUMB'S CATHEDRAL

Scenes from the great Siege of Derry (1688–9) are depicted in stained glass. An audio-visual show relates the siege and outlines the cathedral's history.
Bishop Street Within, Derry. Tel: 028–7126 7313. Open: Monday to Saturday 9am–5pm (to 4pm November to February). Admission charge.

CO ANTRIM
ANDREW JACKSON CENTRE

The parents of the seventh US President emigrated from Carrickfergus in 1765. This 18th-century thatched cottage stands on the site of their original home, and has living quarters, store rooms and stables all under one roof. Graphic displays and a video cover the background to the Ulster-American emigration.
Boneybefore, Carrickfergus. Tel:028–9336 6455. Open: April to October, Monday to Friday 10am–1pm, 2–4pm, weekends 2–4pm; open to 6pm June to September. Admission charge.

CARRICK-A-REDE ROPE BRIDGE

From April to September visitors can cross a bridge here, constructed by local fishermen from planks of wood and wire, which spans the distance between the

Historical figures haunt Carrickfergus Castle

St Columb's Stone, Derry

Information panels have been set up along four marked walks to help visitors interpret the astonishing formations. The National Trust visitor centre has fascinating displays of the region's geology, flora and fauna, and local history exhibits.

Port-na-Spaniagh, a short walk east of the Causeway, is the site of the wrecked Spanish Armada treasure ship *Girona*. *Causeway Head, 3km north of Bushmills on the B146. Tel: 028–2073 1159 (2073 1855 – visitor centre). Causeway freely accessible (a minibus with wheelchair access runs daily from the visitor centre). Centre open: July to August, daily 10am–7pm (earlier closing rest of year). Admission charge for car park, the audio-visual show and minibus.*

mainland and Rathlin Island, a frightening 24 metres above ground. *Off B15, 8km west of Ballycastle. Tel: 028–2076 2178. Bridge: daily 10am–6pm (to 8pm in summer). Visitor centre: May, weekends and public holidays 1–5pm (daily in summer). Car park charge.*

CARRICKFERGUS CASTLE
Northern Ireland's largest, best preserved Norman castle was begun by John de Courcy in 1180. Displays feature life in the castle throughout its history. *Marine Highway, Carrickfergus. Tel: 028–9335 1273. Open: April to September, Monday to Saturday 10am–6pm, Sunday 2–6pm; October to March, Monday to Saturday 10am–4pm, Sunday 2–4pm. Last admission 30 minutes before closing. Admission charge.*

GIANT'S CAUSEWAY
A World Heritage Site, the Causeway consists of 40,000 hexagonal basalt columns – an incredible freak of nature.

KNIGHT RIDE AND HERITAGE PLAZA
Monorail cars, in the shape of Norman helmets, take visitors on a tour of 1,000 years of Carrickfergus history. *Antrim Street, Carrickfergus. Tel: 028–9336 6455. Open: April to September, Monday to Saturday 10am–6pm, Sunday noon–6pm (to 5pm in winter). Last admission 30 minutes before closing. Admission charge.*

OLD BUSHMILLS DISTILLERY
Established in 1608, Bushmills is the world's oldest licensed distillery. Visitors are taken on a one-hour guided tour to see how the famous whiskey is produced – and are rewarded with a tot. *Distillery Road, Bushmills. Tel: 028–2073 1521 (ask for tours department). Open: April to October, Monday to Saturday 9.30am–5.30pm, Sunday noon–5.30pm (last tour 4pm); November to March, Monday to Friday, tours 10.30, 11.30am, 1.30, 2.30 and 3.30pm. Admission charge.*

Belfast's Golden Mile

The area between Donegall Square and Shaftesbury Square is known as the Golden Mile, but it covers less than half a mile (0.8km) and the adjective owes more to commercial success than appearance. Nevertheless, this is a lively part of the city, full of interest. *Allow 1½ hours.*

Start at Donegall Square.

1 DONEGALL SQUARE

Near by

5 Royal Belfast Academic Institution

The eastern and western sides of the square form the terminus for city buses. The square itself is dominated by the massive City Hall (see page 97), and surrounded by the statues of civic worthies, including Sir Edward Harland, founder of the shipyard, Harland and Wolff. Queen Victoria gazes haughtily towards Donegall Place. Number 17 Donegall Square North is the Linen Hall Library, formerly a linen warehouse – note the carved linen drapery across the porch. The Scottish Provident Building in Donegall Square West, another huge edifice, is decorated with looms, ships, spinning wheels and ropes, symbols of Belfast's traditional industries. Yorkshire House, at No 10 Donegall Square South, features the carved heads of Homer, Shakespeare, Schiller, Michaelangelo and George Washington. *At the square's southwest corner follow Bedford Street.*

2 BEDFORD STREET

In the 19th century this was the centre of the city's linen industry and the street was dominated by warehouses. Many have now disappeared. Among the survivors are the palatial Ewart Buildings (Nos 7–17) and the Venetian-style

Built in classical style, City Hall's dome has echoes of St Paul's Cathedral, London

Bryson House at No 28. Ulster Hall, opened in 1861, was intended for grand social occasions but became a focal point for 19th-century political rallies addressed by the likes of Lloyd George and Charles Stewart Parnell. Further on is the BBC Building and a fountain erected as a memorial to a 19th-century physician who died after tireless service at the Home for Incurables.
Bear right into Dublin Road.

3 DUBLIN ROAD
Dublin Road begins with an abundance of furniture shops and furnishing companies, and ends with shops selling second-hand books, stamps and prints. At No 49, opposite the Salvation Army's public relations department, is The Elbow, a popular pub with a plush, intimate atmosphere.
Continue into Shaftesbury Square.

4 SHAFTESBURY SQUARE
Shaftesbury Square marks the beginning of Belfast's student quarter – Queen's University (see page 98) is near by – with lots of small shops and good eating places. Formed by the conjunction of six major thoroughfares, it is Belfast's equivalent of Piccadilly Circus or Times Square. The two supine figures

decorating the façade of the Ulster Bank are known locally as 'Draft' and 'Overdraft'. Next to the post office, on the east side, is Donegall Pass, one of six wide avenues laid across the 17th-century estate of the third Earl of Donegall.
From the west side of Shaftesbury Square walk north along Great Victoria Street.

5 GREAT VICTORIA STREET
Once fashionably residential, this is now a commercial thoroughfare undergoing re-development. It consists mainly of record shops, second-hand bookshops, charity shops and ethnic restaurants. Its stars, however, are the Crown Liquor Saloon and the Grand Opera House, the first opposite and the second alongside the Europa Hotel. Built around 1885, the Crown is a wild extravagance of brilliant tiles, stained glass and panelled snugs – all intimately lit by gas lamps and restored by the National Trust (see page 98).

The Grand Opera House, another recent restoration, was opened in 1895 and now presents a wide-ranging programme (see page 98).
Continue into Fisherwick Place, then College Square East, turning right into Wellington Place to complete the walk back at Donegall Square North.

Belfast's Shopping Area

The city centre north of Donegall Square is Belfast's major shopping precinct, with many large stores and shopping malls. Largely pedestrianised for security reasons, it has some fascinating side streets and secretive, though not threatening, alleys. *Allow 1½ hours.*

Begin at Donegall Square North and proceed northwards along Donegall Place.

1 DONEGALL PLACE

Belfast's Victorian prosperity is reflected in the solid, ornate architecture of the office buildings and stores in Donegall

Near by

❶ Linen Hall Library

❶ City Hall (see page 97)

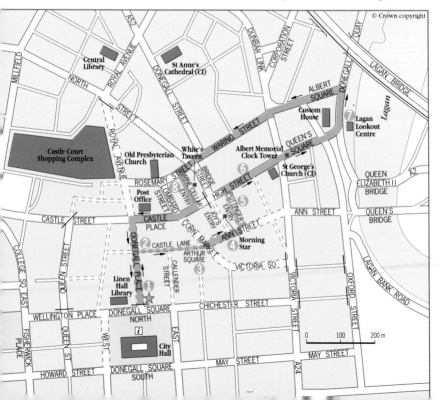

© Crown copyright

Place. Notable examples are the pink sandstone Marks & Spencer building, a linen warehouse when it was erected in 1869; and the copper domes of the former Robinson and Cleaver store, with a carved façade featuring some of the company's distinguished customers.
Turn right into Castle Lane.

2 CASTLE LANE

Halfway along this pleasantly pedestrianised lane, on the right, is Callender Street, the main depot for pressing, weighing and packing linen in the late 18th century. Callendering is the smoothing process that gives bleached linen its final sheen.
Continue to Arthur Square.

3 ARTHUR SQUARE

The city's oldest square is named after Sir Arthur Chichester, the Elizabethan adventurer who received Belfast as a reward in 1603 for defeating the great Hugh O'Neill. With its bandstand, clock and buskers, the square today is a relaxing spot for shoppers.
Cross the square directly and enter Ann Street.

4 ANN STREET

Ann Street allows a glimpse of 19th-century Belfast, when half the city's streets were small courts and 'entries' – narrow alleyways. Half a dozen of these can be seen on the left. Joy's Entry carries the name of the family that published Britain's first daily newspaper, the *Belfast News Letter*, in 1737.
Turn left into Pottinger's Entry.

5 POTTINGER'S ENTRY

This was a fashionable address in the 1820s when the entry had 34 houses. Today it contains one of Belfast's

classical saloon bars, the Morning Star, with its frosted-glass windows and polished interior of mahogany and brass.
Turn right into High Street.

6 HIGH STREET

On the corner of High Street and Victoria Street is the imposing Protestant church of St George's, completed in 1816. Its splendid portico came from a palatial house that was intended as a home for Frederick Hervey, Earl Bishop of Derry, but when he died the house was dismantled and the portico moved to St George's. The nearby Albert Memorial Clock Tower tilts some 1.3m from the vertical as a result of poor foundations. The tower was erected in 1865 and the tilt was noticed as long ago as 1901.
Cross Victoria Street to Queen's Square and on to Donegall Quay.

7 DONEGALL QUAY

The large yellow Italianate building overlooking the river is Custom House, built between 1854 and 1857 by Sir Charles Lanyon, architect of many of Belfast's Victorian buildings. Near by a recently constructed weir across the River Lagan can be viewed from the Lagan Lookout Centre (see page 98).
From Donegall Quay turn left into Albert Square and continue into Waring Street. Cross Bridge Street to Rosemary Street and turn left into Wine Cellar Entry.

8 WINE CELLAR ENTRY

Here is the city's oldest pub, White's Tavern, opened in 1630 and re-built in 1790. An open fire and plush seating contribute to a welcoming atmosphere.
Continue to High Street, turning right into Castle Place. At Donegall Place turn left to return to the walk's starting point.

Fermanagh Lakeland

Fermanagh is an area of stunning beauty, with lakes and mountains, mysterious islands and enigmatic hints at a pagan past. *Allow 1 day.*

Begin at Enniskillen.

1 ENNISKILLEN

Near by

4 Lough Navar Forest (see page 110)

Enniskillen straddles the River Erne which connects Upper and Lower Lough Erne. Watergate, part of the old castle, now houses the Fermanagh County Museum and the Regimental Museum of the Royal Inniskilling Fusiliers (see page 110).

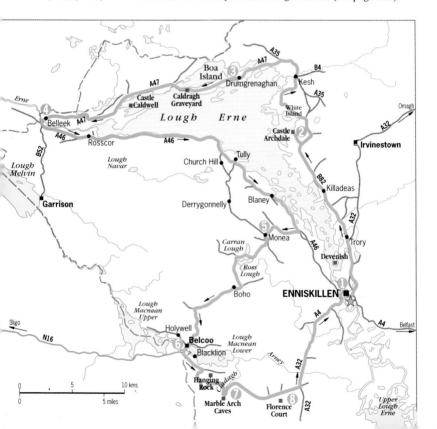

Oscar Wilde and Samuel Beckett were both old boys of Portora Royal School.

From the village of Trory, 5km north of Enniskillen, a ferry runs across to Devenish Island (see page 109).

Take the A32 for 3km, then the B82 for 11km, turning off to Castle Archdale.

2 CASTLE ARCHDALE

The marina, caravan site and youth hostel can make this a busy place, but tranquillity can be found in the surrounding country park. The estate has a butterfly park, an arboretum and rare breeds of farm animals. The ruins of an old castle, razed in 1689, can be seen in the forest (see page 109).

White Island, with strange stone figures in a ruined church, can be reached by boat from Castle Archdale. *Turn left on the B82 and after 3km leave the B road and follow the scenic route for 6km to Kesh, then turn left on to the A35 for 1.5km before taking the A47 for 13km to Boa Island.*

3 BOA ISLAND

Towards the far end of the island, watch for a sign to Caldragh Graveyard on the left. Park at the roadside and prepare for a possibly muddy walk of about 1km. At the end of the concrete track an overgrown old graveyard contains two uncanny stone figures among its unkempt tombstones. A double-faced Janus is smiling on one side, scowling on the other, while beside him a small hunched figure leers disconcertingly. Both figures evoke uneasy echoes of pre-Christian Ireland. *Continue on the A47 for 16km to Belleek.*

4 BELLEEK

A border village, Belleek is famed for its fine basketwork china (see pages 108–9).

Take the A46 for Enniskillen and after 33km turn right and follow the signs to Monea.

5 MONEA

Monea is a ruined 17th-century castle, built by 'planters' from Scotland. It was captured by the Irish in 1641 and abandoned in 1750. An ancient *crannog* – artificial island dwelling – can be traced in the marsh in front of Monea. *Turn left leaving Monea, then left again for Enniskillen. Turn right, following signs for Boho for 8km, then turn right for Belcoo.*

6 BELCOO

Noted for its first-class coarse fishing, Belcoo sits between Upper and Lower Lough Macnean. Just north of the village is the Holywell, a shrine for pilgrims.

Cross into the Republic at Blacklion for a short distance, then cross back into Northern Ireland. Follow the south shore of Lower Lough Macnean. Turn right along Marlbank Scenic Loop and drive for 5km to Marble Arch.

7 MARBLE ARCH CAVES

Electric boats take visitors on a tour of this spectacular underground system of caverns and chasms. There is an excellent visitor centre and the surrounding countryside is beautiful (see page 110).

Turn left, then right, and drive for 6km to Florence Court.

8 FLORENCE COURT

A grand Anglo-Irish mansion, Florence Court was built in the early 18th century and named in honour of a new English wife (see page 110).

Return to Enniskillen by the A32 and the A4.

Legends and the Little People

*A*ll over Ireland you can see farm gates standing between sturdy stone posts with conical caps. The gateposts are this shape (would you believe it?) to discourage the Little People from sitting about on them for too long. At the same time, nobody wants to offend them by disturbing a mound in a field, where they are believed to live. Dreadful disaster could follow.

The hawthorn or Fairy Tree, should never be interfered with, either. Bad luck will result, probably in the form of sickness affecting livestock.

Ireland is steeped in superstition and folklore, handed down through the generations. The Banshee is greatly feared. Some families, it seems, are haunted by this fairy, which wails and keens when a death is imminent.

Leprechauns – little men in green tunics – are reputed to sit under trees mending fairies' shoes. Leprechauns (the *Oxford Dictionary* calls them 'small mischievous sprites') are said to possess a crock of gold. Any mortal who can stare at a Leprechaun gets the crock, but if his gaze wavers for an instant, the treasure disappears.

One of the best-known legends concerns the four children of Lír, whose jealous stepmother had them turned into swans for 400 years. The sentence is now long passed, and the four died as ancient humans, but to this day it is illegal to kill swans.

Tales are told of legendary heroes like Cuchulain, The Hound of Ulster, who fought off an invading army single-handed with his javelin.

The lucky Irish shamrock turns up wherever St Patrick's Day is celebrated throughout the world. St Patrick used it to illustrate the story of the Holy Trinity.

In a land of legend and superstition it is fitting that University College, Dublin, should have a Department of Folklore, where a huge collection of documents, pictures and tapes records every aspect of the subject.

The legendary Children of Lír – condemned to live their lives as swans

GETTING AWAY FROM IT ALL

'O Ireland, isn't it grand you look –
Like a bride in her rich adornin'?
And with all the pent-up love of my heart
I bid you top o' the mornin'!'
JOHN LOCKE, 1847–89

BEACHES

Most people who know Ireland well will argue that simply being there is getting away from it all. Generally, there is such a laid-back atmosphere about the country that few visitors shoulder the burden of care for long. Those seeking solitude may have to travel a little further than the rest, for the Irish are a gregarious people – but quiet places there are in abundance.

There is no shortage of beaches along Ireland's shoreline. Many are as beautiful as you will find anywhere in the world, ranging from long stretches of deserted dunes to intimate rocky coves.

LEINSTER

Close to Dublin, on the DART system, Dalkey and Killiney (pronounced 'Dorkee' and 'Kill-aye-nee') are attractive spots for a half-day's outing. Dalkey has narrow streets and elegant

houses. Boat trips can be taken during the summer to Dalkey Island, which has a bird sanctuary and a Martello tower. Killiney, set in a sweeping bay with neat villas, lush gardens and two Sugarloaf mountains, is often compared with the Bay of Naples.

Courtown, Co Wexford, is a pleasant harbour village 40km north of Wexford Town. Its 3km-long sandy beach, amusements and golf course make it a popular family resort. Also in Co Wexford, Kilmore Quay, about 19km southwest of Rosslare, is a pretty fishing village with excellent beaches.

MUNSTER

Ardmore, Co Waterford, is a charming resort with a good beach at the base of a cliff. About 21km southwest of Dungarvan, it has impressive monastic ruins surrounding an almost intact round tower.

Birdwatchers will be attracted to Castlegregory, Co Kerry, on the western shore of Tralee Bay. The beaches are superb, and many unusual species – including Bewick's swans – have been logged at the nearby Lough Gill bird sanctuary.

Dunmore East, Co Waterford, is a delightful village of thatched cottages and friendly pubs overlooking a picturesque bay and fishing harbour 16km south of Waterford. Its sandy beaches are protected by rose-hued cliffs.

Lahinch is the busiest resort in Co Clare, but there is still plenty of room along its splendid beach and nearby dunes. The surfing is good and there is a championship golf course.

Courtown Bay, a popular family resort with its superb 3km stretch of sand

Ireland's beaches are as beautiful and varied as any you will find in the world. This one is at Dingle

CONNACHT

Some 100km northwest of Galway City, Roundstone is a relaxing, pretty village resort on the edge of a bay, and has become a popular summer resort. First settled by Scottish fishermen in the 19th century, today it has a community of artists and crafts folk whose workshops may be visited.

Spiddall, 19km west of Galway, has a well-named beach in the Silver Strand. There is good shore fishing, and in the summer there are exciting races between *currachs*, the traditional canvas-skinned boats.

Eight kilometres west of Sligo, Strandhill is a favoured place for surfing championships. For those who prefer quieter waters, Culleenamore, round the corner in Ballysadare Bay, is the place.

ULSTER

Standing on a beautiful beach on Lough Swilly, Rathmullen in Co Donegal has a ruined 16th-century priory and an informative heritage centre. It is also the start of the Fanad Drive, with even more wonderful beaches, as well as streams, lakes and mountains.

Cushendun, Co Antrim, was built in the style of a Cornish village – a tribute by Lord Cushendun to his Cornish wife. There is a good beach, and from nearby Torr Head you can see Scotland's Mull of Kintyre.

Newcastle, Co Down, is where 'the Mountains of Mourne sweep down to the sea'. A traditional and popular resort, it has a magnificent sandy beach. Towering 852m above the town is Slieve Donard.

Dun Aengus prehistoric fort perches on a cliff 90m above the sea on Inishmore

ISLANDS

Storm-battered or bathed in sunshine, obscured by mist or magnified in the strange light of a rainbow sky, the islands of Ireland beckon with a promise of rugged freedom.

Most of the islands lie within 8km of the mainland and none is more than 16km out. Each has been inhabited at some time – the wildest by no more than a hermit monk or two in the early days of Christianity. Celtic crosses, ruined chapels and dwellings are everywhere. A few are still inhabited.

Facilities are few, but the islanders extend a warm hospitality to visitors. There are a few family-run hotels and guesthouses.

THE NORTH

Five kilometres off the coast of Donegal, **Aran Island** is served by a ferry from Burtonport. The island is hilly, with rough moorland and cliffs on the Atlantic side, and sandy beaches and rock pools facing the mainland. Seven pubs and a hotel set the pace of the island's social life.

Rathlin, off the north coast of Co Antrim, is home to 30 families, mostly involved in raising sheep and cattle. Settled originally by early Christian monks, Rathlin has suffered plunder, piracy and massacre. The cave in which Robert the Bruce studied a resolute spider can be visited in good weather. The island has a bird sanctuary, a diving centre, three lighthouses and a pub. The crossing from Ballycastle takes about 50 minutes.

THE WEST

The three **Aran Islands** – Inishmore, Inishmaan and Inisheer – dominate the horizon off the coasts of Clare and Galway. Like The Burren, the islands consist mainly of bare, grey limestone scoured by Ice Age glaciers. But the bleakness is tempered by stone-walled pastures and wild flowers.

Inishmore, the largest, has 14 small villages and a fishing harbour at Kilronan. Dún Aengus is the largest of several prehistoric forts and there are many early Christian churches, including 7th-century St Benan's.

Inishmaan has two impressive prehistoric forts and the cottage in which the writer J M Synge lived.

Inisheer, southernmost of the islands, has narrow roads and a gleaming white beach on which *currachs* are built.

Rising to a height of some 500m in Clew Bay, Co Mayo, **Clare Island** will appeal to walkers. It also offers fishing, sailboarding, pony trekking and diving. Clare's wildlife includes dolphins, seals and otters and it is also home to the chough, a rare, red-billed crow. A square tower near the harbour was the stronghold of Grace O'Malley, the 16th-century pirate who declared herself queen of Clew Bay and held her own against Elizabeth I on a visit to London in 1575.

THE SOUTHWEST

A cable-car links **Dursey Island** to the mainland off the tip of the Beara Peninsula in Co Cork. Popular with birdwatchers, who climb the western cliffs to observe gannets and search for rare migrants, the island has no paved roads. Transport between the three tiny villages is by motorcycle or horse-drawn vehicle.

Cape Clear, Ireland's southernmost island, challenges the Atlantic from Roaringwater Bay in West Cork. About 5km long, the island is wild and precipitous, but there are tiny pastures

and its houses are protected by hedges of fuchsia and escallonia. During the summer its population of 150 is swollen by the visitors, naturalists and Irish language students who travel by ferries from Schull and Baltimore.

Celtic crosses at dawn on Inishmore, the largest of the Aran Islands

ARAN ISLANDS

There are air services from Inverin, Connemara (tel: 091–593034). Ferries operate from Doolin, Co Clare (tel: 065–74455), Galway City (tel: 091–567676) and Rossaveel, Co Galway (tel: 091–568093). Heritage Centre, Inishmore (tel: 091–563081 for hours). Inishmaan and Inisheer are traffic free.

CLARE ISLAND

A regular ferry service operates from Roonah Pier, near Louisburg (tel: 098–26307). Trips take 15 minutes.

DURSEY ISLAND

Cable-car – tel: 027–73017.

CAPE CLEAR

Ferries: Schull – tel: 028–28138
        Baltimore – tel: 028–39119.

WATERWAYS

You don't have to drive very far in Ireland before encountering a lough (lake) or river. But why drive? Both the Republic and Northern Ireland offer alternatives in the form of waterway holidays. Vital in the days before the railways, the waterways have become a rich legacy of leisure, affording a relaxing opportunity to gain a backyard view of Ireland at its best.

The Republic has three major waterway systems, each connected to the other. From Dublin, the Grand Canal runs westwards to meet the stately River Shannon. Less than halfway along its route, a branch of the canal goes off to meet the River Barrow, which provides a navigable route south to St Mullins before reaching the sea at Waterford.

Northern Ireland has Lough Erne – Upper and Lower – a superb lakeland cruising area, with an island, they'll tell you, for every day of the year.

Thanks to restoration work on a

GRAND CANAL
Celtic Canal Cruisers, Tullamore, Co Offaly (tel: 0506–21861), offers English-style narrowboats for hire.

RIVER SHANNON
Ten companies offer nearly 400 self-skippered boats for hire on the Shannon. Details in *Ireland's Magic Waterways* available from Bord Fáilte offices (see page 189).

RIVER BARROW
Celtic Canal Cruisers – see **Grand Canal** above.

LOUGH ERNE
Fermanagh Tourist Information Centre, Wellington Road, Enniskillen, Co Fermanagh (tel: 028–6632 3110).

Clonmacnois monastic settlement on the banks of the mighty River Shannon

derelict canal, the Shannon-Erne Waterway now connects the River Shannon with Lough Erne, enabling boaters to cruise freely over some 800km between the provinces of Leinster, Munster and Ulster.

THE GRAND CANAL

Between Lucan, just outside Dublin, and Shannon Harbour there are only 36 locks in a distance of about 130km. Robertstown, where the River Barrow link starts, is an attractive village with a boating centre and a base for hiring cruisers. Edenderry, on a spur off the canal's main line, has excellent moorings in a pretty harbour. Tullamore is the home of *Tullamore Dew* whiskey and the liqueur, *Irish Mist*. Shannon Harbour, marking the entrance to Ireland's major river, was once a thriving inland port. It now provides a safe haven for many boaters.

RIVER SHANNON

The Shannon contains the largest area of inland waters in Britain and Ireland. It flows southwards for 350km, following the course of history between Co Cavan, where it rises, and the Atlantic Ocean. It passes through only one city – Limerick – but it provides an opportunity to view and visit some of Ireland's finest historical sites, including the stunning Clonmacnois (see pages 50–1), the most important early Christian monastic settlement. Carrick-on-Shannon, a popular starting point for cruising holidays, has some fine Georgian buildings.

Along its length, the Shannon has a wealth of birdlife and flora, and it is flanked by ancient woodlands. There are nature trails to explore at Portumna Castle, on the shore of Lough Derg, and in Lough Key Forest Park.

What a catch! Fishing at Lough Erne

RIVER BARROW

The river passes through many fascinating places. Athy is a market town whose history goes back to medieval times. Carlow has a Norman castle. Graiguenamanagh is a photogenic town with the restored Duiske Abbey, founded in 1207. St Mullins, near the end of the navigation, has associations with early Celtic mythology.

LOUGH ERNE

Cruising offers the best way to see many of Fermanagh's attractions. Mooring up at Devenish and White Islands, for example, enables you to view their mysterious ruins and relics without the crowds. Devenish is wonderful by moonlight (see page 109). Navigation throughout the Erne system is easy and boating facilities are excellent.

HIKING AND CYCLING

Great country for walking and cycling, in mountain, forest, glen and valley, can be found throughout Ireland. The Ulster Way, an 800km circular footpath, follows the Northern Ireland coastline, returning to Belfast through the Sperrin Mountains, the Fermanagh Lakeland and the Mountains of Mourne.

In the Republic there are 27 marked trails, over 2,750km in all, ranging from the Burren Way (35km) to Bealach na Gaeltachta (387km). Details are found in the Irish Tourist Board's brochure, *Walking Ireland – the Waymarked Ways*.

Some organised walks have a base, with daily walks. Post-to-post walking is available in some areas with luggage transported from base to base.

Hikers' accommodation can usually be found near trails. Most farmers allow overnight camping if asked. Self-guided trails or guided walks are available in Ireland's national parks.

Most of Ireland's roads, being relatively free of motor traffic, are a joy for cyclists, and many areas are ideal for all-terrain bikes, which can be hired in the north and south.

> **INFORMATION**
> **Ulster Way** Sports Council for Northern Ireland, House of Sport, Malone Road, Belfast BT9 5LA (tel: 028–9038 1222).
> **National Waymarked Ways Committee**
> Department of Tourism, Sports and Recreation, Frederick Buildings, South Frederick Street, Dublin 2 (tel: 01–662 1444).
> **Federation of Irish Cyclists**
> Kelly Roche House, 619 North Circular Road, Dublin 1 (tel: 01–855 1522).
> **Walking/Cycling Ireland**
> Mespil House, Sussex Road, Dublin 4 (tel: 01–668 8278).

Specialists who arrange walking and cycling holidays, with or without a guide, are listed in the Irish Tourist Board's brochure *Walking/Cycling Ireland*.

Ireland is a marvellous country for walking, hiking and rambling

DIRECTORY

'In some parts of Ireland
the sleep which knows
no waking is always
followed by the wake
which knows no sleeping.'
MARY WILSON LITTLE

Shopping

*M*any of the souvenirs on sale to visitors are bought at shops within craft centres, factories and mills, after they have seen the goods at various stages of production. Some of these shops stock a range of products made elsewhere in Ireland. Good quality mementoes and gifts are also on sale at Tourist Offices.

Both Belfast and Dublin have compact city centres. Both cities have some splendid multi-floor, covered shopping centres – among them Westbury Mall and the Powerscourt Town House Centre in Dublin, and Castle Court in Belfast.

Belfast's waterfront redevelopment scheme includes some up-market shops within a conference centre, concert hall and hotel complex.

Belfast is the traditional home of Irish linen, and this can be found in several of the city's arcades and pedestrianised area shops. Handmade woollens, pottery and glassware – Tyrone Crystal is made in Ulster (see page 111) – are welcome gifts. The Craftworks shop in the centre of Belfast sells a wide range of locally made crafts while the Smithfield Retail

A shop sign as good as the contents of the window

Market offers a number of small specialised shops under one roof.

In Dublin, pedestrianised Grafton Street and its environs, and wide O'Connell Street, are the main places for the committed shopper, with windows displaying classic clothes and exciting new styles, and designer knitwear. Nearby Nassau Street has a parade of shops, some of which are still in the hands of the families that founded them. Exquisite woollens and tweeds are on sale. One shop sells men's and women's suits, jackets and hats in handwoven Donegal tweed, and lengths of tweed can be bought, so that customers can have them made up when they get home.

Cork City shops are mostly small and interesting, each retailer an expert in his or her field. High quality fashions are elegantly displayed cheek by jowl with bookshops, tobacconists, pharmacies, hardware stores, toy shops and jewellers. Crescent-shaped St Patrick's Street is the main shopping thoroughfare, and a pedestrianised area is flanked by Carey's Lane, French Church Street and Paul Street.

Several craft studios have been set up in the Bridge Mills in Galway, by O'Brien's Bridge. The converted 18th-century mill also houses a wine bar and second-hand bookshop.

Waterford City presents itself as the 'Shopping Capital of the Southeast', and is indeed a vibrant centre with a range of specialist outlets lining its narrow streets.

There are bargains for dedicated shoppers, from books to traditional Irish knitwear

Waterford Crystal heads the field (see page 66), but there are several other centres in which quality crystal is created. Pottery, already firmly established in some areas – Belleek is the best-known (see pages 108–9) – is a developing craft. Studios producing functional and decorative pottery are opening all over the country.

You can still see handmade Irish harps, made in Mayo, Meath and Dublin. Craftsmen in Limerick, Clare and Cork make chairs and stools in local ash or beech. Burnished blackthorn is used for walking sticks. Good examples of the blacksmith's craft – fire irons and ornamental ironwork – are produced in Cork and Kerry.

Jewellery in silver, gold and enamel is created in unusual and classic designs. The famous Claddagh ring – the lovers' symbol of two hands cradling a crowned heart – can be found in sterling silver.

Basket weaving and rushwork are homecrafts producing a variety of goods, including tablemats. Among other crafts practised around the country are batik work – fairly new to Ireland – stained glass, tapestry, fly-tying and leather-work.

A three-week Shopping Spree takes place in Sligo each autumn, with bargains to be had all over town.

Throughout the country many of the shops selling crafts and goods of Irish manufacture run a mailing service.

Visitors from outside the European Union may reclaim the cost of Value Added Tax (VAT) on purchases made in the Republic and Northern Ireland.

SHOPS

Countless shops throughout Ireland offer crafted gifts and souvenirs. There is not the space here to mention more than a few outlets selling Ireland's high quality products. For information on local outlets for a particular purchase inquire at the nearest tourist office.

ANTIQUES
BELFAST
Belfast Antiques Market
Stamps, coins, furniture, toys.
126 Donegall Pass, Belfast 7.
Tel: 028–9023 2041. Saturdays only.

CO ANTRIM
Country Antiques
Silver, porcelain, furniture.
219b Lisnevenagh Road, Antrim.
Tel: 028–9446 2498.

CO CORK
Victoria's
Period clothes, Victoriana.
2 Oliver Plunkett Street, Cork.
Tel: 021–272752.

CO DONEGAL
The Gallery
Paintings, antiques, crafts.
Dunfanaghy. Tel: 074–36224.

CO DUBLIN
Mother Redcap's Indoor Market
Antiques, crafts, paintings and other wares.
Back Lane, Christchurch, Dublin 8.
No telephone.

CO FERMANAGH
Ballindullagh Barn
Curios, crafts and paintings in an off-the-beaten-track 18th-century barn.
Killadeas. Tel: 028–6662 1548.

ART
CO KERRY
Killarney Art Gallery (Mulvany Bros)
The work of Irish painters is on sale here.
47 High Street, Killarney. No telephone.

BOOKS
CO DUBLIN
Easons
Four spacious floors of books, stationery, posters, souvenirs and other goods.
40 O'Connell Street, Dublin 1. Tel: 01–873 3811.

Fred Hanna
Books of Irish interest. Huge range on most subjects.
27–9 Nassau Street, Dublin 2.
Tel: 01– 677 1255.

Hodges Figgis
One and a half million books stocked – if it's not here, the management claims, then it simply does not exist.
56–8 Dawson Street, Dublin 2.
Tel: 01– 677 4754.

Winding Stair
Interesting Liffey-side second-hand book store.
40 Lower Ormond Quay, Dublin 1.
Tel: 01–873 3292.

CRAFTS
BELFAST
Craftworks Gallery
Government-sponsored gallery with a wide range of Northern Ireland crafts on sale.
13 Linenhall Street, Belfast 2.
Tel: 028–9023 6534.

CO CLARE
Gleninagh Crafts
Stained-glass products and unusual items – mobiles, lamps, candle holders.
Fiontrach, Ballyvaughan. Tel: 065–77154.

CO CORK
Blarney Woollen Mills
Much more than woollens – a wide selection of Ireland's goods.
Blarney. Tel: 021–385280. Also 21–3 Nassau Street, Dublin 2.
Tel: 01–671 0068.
Trag Knitwear
Selection of hand- and machine-knit Aran sweaters. Fashions, crafts. Bargain basement.
Tragumna, Skibbereen. Tel: 028–21750.

CO DONEGAL
Magee
Department store. Established 1866. Magee's hand-woven tweed is still made in cottages and finished in the factory. High-grade men's and women's clothing.
The Diamond, Donegal. Tel: 073–21100.
McAuliffe's Craft Shop
Hand-woven rugs. Men's and women's clothes in Irish textiles. Crystal.
Dunfanaghy. Tel: 074–36135.
Teresa's Cottage Industries
Embroidered table linen, luncheon sets and cushion covers. Place mats, bed linens, knitwear.
Church Street View, Bruckless.
Tel: 073–37080.
Triona Fashions
Weaving demonstrations. Factory shop. Ladies' fashions in tweed; other Irish products.
Ardara. Tel: 075–41422.

CO DUBLIN
Gaelic Design Sweater & Gift Shop
Souvenirs from Guinness boxer shorts to *bodhrans* (small, single-skin drums). Also classy cottons, tweeds and other knitwear.
Asdills Row, Temple Bar, Dublin 2.
Tel: 01–671 1146.

Whichcraft
Contemporary craftwork from all over Ireland.
5 Castlegate, Lord Edward Street, Dublin.
Tel: 01–670 9371.

CO KERRY
Quill's Woollen Market
Claims the best selection of designer handknits and woollen goods – and keenest prices. Also in Sneem and Kenmare.
Killarney. Tel: 064–32277.

CO SLIGO
Innisfree Crystal
Many limited editions which can only be purchased at the factory.
The Bridge, Collooney. Tel: 071–667340.

CO WATERFORD
Waterford Design Centre
Three floors of traditional crafts, giftware and clothes.
44 The Quay, Waterford.
Tel: 051–856666.

JEWELLERY
CO DONEGAL
McElwee
Crystal from Waterford, Tipperary and Derryveagh. China and ironstone ware. Rynhart bronze sculptures.
Dungloe. Tel: 075–21032.

CO SLIGO
The Cat & The Moon
Hand-crafted silver and gold. Work by other Irish artists.
Castle Street, Sligo. Tel: 071–43686.
W F Henry
Large range of jewellery and watches, including Claddagh rings in gold and silver.
1 High Street, Sligo. Tel: 071–42658.

TEXTILE CRAFTS

Crafts usually develop where the raw materials are available. It follows, therefore, that homespun tweeds and woollens were traditionally based in noted sheep-rearing areas like Donegal, Galway, Kerry, Mayo and Wicklow. Each region had its distinctive product, depending not only on the local wool used, but also on the local dyes.

In parts of Donegal, long famous for its strong tweed, hand-weaving continues as a cottage industry. The crafts of hand knitting and hand embroidery are still found here. In the same areas, workshops can be visited where a new generation of weavers produces lighter, brighter textiles – scarves, dress lengths, rugs and wall hangings.

Aran jerseys are never out of fashion, though they owe their origin to the fact that they are practical – thick, warm and rain-resistant – and

Ireland has a reputation for excellent quality textiles, many produced using the time-honoured traditional ways

process in linen manufacturing. Wellbrook Beetling Mill, near Cookstown, Co Tyrone, opens for limited hours on summer afternoons and is well worth a visit (see page 112).

The Middle House Museum, at Upperlands, Maghera, Co Londonderry, has a private textile museum opened by appointment by the Clark family, who live there. The machinery dates from 1740 (tel: 028–7964 2214) to arrange a guided tour).

Yarn was bleached by boiling, and laid out to dry on 'bleach greens'. Northern Ireland had about 360 bleach greens in the industry's late 18th-century heyday.

ideal for wintry sea fishing trips in an open boat. Even the intricate patterns devised by families and passed down from one generation to the next were rooted in practicality, if a somewhat morbid one. It is said they were a means of identifying drowned fishermen.

Irish hand crochet work is a much sought-after fashion accessory today.

Weaving in linen is now limited to Northern Ireland. A little flax is still grown there, but most is imported. Beetling – hammering the cloth to produce a smooth sheen – is the final

Entertainment

*I*reland does not immediately spring to mind when planning a holiday with a sizzling nightlife, but you would be wrong to dismiss it altogether.

Much of the nightlife is impromptu. A lot of it takes place in pubs and bars; places where people know they can relax over a drink in pleasant company, chat with acquaintances or strangers, and where there is always a chance of someone striking up a tune on a tin whistle, a guitar or fiddle, or even the uilleann pipes. And suddenly there's a sing-song, a 'session' they call it.

This is the 'crack', the good-time fun factor, and if you don't want strong drink you can get it with tea or coffee. To go to Ireland and not visit the bars is as unthinkable as going to Egypt without seeing the pyramids.

But if you want organised entertainment, the best you can expect outside Dublin, Belfast and the main centres is the cinema, bingo, bowling, possibly an evening of amateur folk dancing in a local hall, or a disco where anyone over

Dublin's National Concert Hall – a magnificent setting for musical performances

30 may be considered geriatric.

The answer for those wanting to dance until dawn, to take in a night at the opera or theatre, or to hear a top-class rock band or international orchestra is to come to Ireland in July or August. They do get big-name, high calibre entertainment here, but it may not coincide with a visit outside the peak holiday season.

To find out what is on, keep an eye on the local newspapers which carry advertising and editorial information on entertainments taking place in the area. For more detailed news of what to see and do call at the tourist information office. Apart from leaflets on local attractions and festivals, free newspaper-style publications, such as the *Cork and Kerry Tourist News* and the *Northern Ireland Holiday News*, are a mine of information.

Entire regions, like the Northwest (Cavan, Donegal, Leitrim, Monaghan and Sligo) and Shannon (Clare, Limerick, North Kerry, North Tipperary and South Offaly) are covered in annual visitors' guides. Many small towns have a privately published free sheet, like the *Tralee Advertiser*.

In Northern Ireland, the 20-page *Lakeland Extra* is distributed to homes and businesses in Fermanagh and South Tyrone, and can also be picked up at

The Manhattan night club, Belfast, where you can dance the night away

various locations, including tourist information centres.

There is every chance you will find something of interest in these publications, but don't expect it to keep you riveted until the small hours. You could be in bed by 10pm.

The advice given in one of the free monthly papers for visitors is: 'Rest well to prepare for another day of fun and adventure in the region that nature has indeed given more than its fair share.' And why should anyone argue with that?

Apart from the minute terrorist fraternity on both sides of the community, the Irish are a friendly, welcoming people. Nobody who seeks company is allowed to be lonely in Ireland.

It is not that they are curious about you. They are not nosy. They do not intrude. They just recognise you are someone to talk to, and the talk is never trite or tedious. It is straight from the heart, it is anecdotal, informative, showing interest in your responses, your impressions of Ireland and the Irish. It leads to humour, wit and laughter, it extends to others in your proximity – be it at bus stop or bar – and suddenly you are enjoying yourself enormously.

WHAT'S ON

Many of the entertainments listed here take place only during the summer, and others, like live music in pubs, are limited to fewer appearances. It is wise to check beforehand.

AMUSEMENT CENTRES

See page 150.

BANQUETS

CO CLARE

Bunratty Castle
Twice-nightly medieval banquet year round.
Bunratty. Tel: 061–61788 for reservations.
Bunratty Folk Park Ceilidh Evenings
Irish stew and traditional Irish singing and dancing.
Bunratty. Tel: 061–61788 for reservations.
Knappogue Castle
Twice-nightly medieval banquets with musical entertainment from May to October.
Quin. Tel: 061–61788 for reservations.

CO GALWAY

Dunguaire Castle Medieval Banquet
Extracts from works of Synge, Yeats and Gogarty. Twice nightly (times: 5.30 and 8.45pm) May to September.
Kinvara. Tel: 061–61788 for reservations.

CO KERRY

Killarney Manor
Five-course banquet with Irish music, song and dance in 18th-century Great Hall.
Loreto Road, Killarney. Tel: 064–31551.

CO OFFALY

Kinitty Castle
Medieval banquets, June to September, Tuesday and Wednesday at 7pm.
Kinitty, Birr. Tel: 0509–37318.

BOWLING

CO LIMERICK

Limerick Leisure Bowl
Twenty computerised lanes. Gym, sauna and dance classes.
Ennis Road, Limerick. Tel: 061–327444.

CO WATERFORD

Clonea Strand Hotel
Bowling alley.
Dungarvan. Tel: 058–42416.

CABARET

BELFAST

Limelight
Disco/nightclub. Cabaret Tuesday, Friday and Saturday.
17 Ormeau Avenue. No telephone.

CO DUBLIN

Abbey Tavern
Fun, laughter and traditional singing.
Howth. Tel: 01–839 0307.
Braemor Rooms
Home-reared stars and some from the world stage.
County Club Churchtown, Dublin 14. Tel: 01–296 0685.
Jury's Irish Cabaret
Sparkling 2½-hour entertainment, May to October.
Jury's Hotel, Pembroke Road, Ballsbridge, Dublin 4. Tel: 01–660 5000.
Renard's
Piano and jazz bar with live music until late, Wednesday to Saturday.
33–5 South Frederick Street, Dublin 2. Tel: 01– 677 5876.

CO LIMERICK

Jury's Hotel
A variety of acts at Jury's Summer Show: Thursday nights, June to September, also Wednesdays, July and August.
Ennis Road, Limerick. Tel: 061–327777.

CONCERTS AND OPERA
BELFAST
Grand Opera House
See pages 98 and 145.
Queens University School of Music
Admission charge for evening concerts.
Free lunchtime recitals autumn/winter.
University Square/Botanic Avenue. Tel: 028–9024 5133, ext 3480, for information.
Ulster Orchestra
Ulster Hall, Bedford Street. Tel: 028–9032 3900 for ticket information.

CO CORK
Cork Opera House
Irish plays predominate in summer.
Opera, ballet, musical comedy.
Lavitt's Quay, Cork. Tel: 021–270022.

CO DUBLIN
National Concert Hall
Leading venue for classical music.
Earlsfort Terrace, Dublin 2. Tel: 01– 475 1572.

CO LONDONDERRY
Guildhall
Concerts and dramatic productions.
Shipquay Street, Londonderry.
Tel: 028–7136 5151.

HOTEL ENTERTAINMENT
CO CLARE
Bunratty Castle Hotel
Garfield's Cabaret and Niteclub open to the small hours Friday and Saturday.
Bunratty. Tel: 061–364116.
Lakeside Hotel and Leisure Centre
Cast of talented singers, musicians, step-dancers and comedians in cabaret. Late June to early September.
Killaloe. Tel: 061–376122.
West County Conference and Leisure Hotel
Ballads, step-dancing, drama and comedy in cabaret: Tuesdays in June, Tuesday and Friday, July to September.
Ennis. Tel: 065–682300.

CO DUBLIN
Harcourt Hotel
Former home of George Bernard Shaw.
Traditional Irish music nightly and G B Shaws Restaurant.
60–1 Harcourt Street, Dublin 2.
Tel: 01–478 3677.

CO GALWAY
Peacocke's
Irish Night Saturdays, disco Friday and Sunday 10pm–2am.
Maam Cross. Tel: 091–552306.

CO KERRY
Ballybunion Golf Hotel
Baby-sitting service. Nightly entertainment.
Main Street, Ballybunion.
Tel: 068–27111.
Eviston House Hotel
Danny Mann Singing Lounge, Scoundrels Niteclub.
New Street, Killarney. Tel: 064–31640.
Gleneagle Hotel
Wings Nightclub with top names.
Nightly music and sing-along in summer at Eagles Whistle pub.
Muckross Road, Killarney.
Tel: 064–31870.
Killarney Towers Hotel and Leisure Centre
Scruffy's Music Bar nightly.
College Square, Killarney. Tel: 064–31038.

CO LIMERICK
Royal George Hotel
Tropics Nightclub, open nightly, and Glory Hole Music Pub.
O'Connell Street, Limerick.
Tel: 061–414566.

THE PUBS

People rave about Ireland's pubs and bars – the 'crack' (conversation and good-time factor), the character, the generally easy-going ambience. And justifiably. That is not to say, however, that some of them don't have dismal décor, plastic upholstery and archaic fittings.

The trouble is, most have frosted windows or are heavily curtained, so you can't tell what they're like until you go in. However, at least three times out of four you'll be successful, and even the dreary ones usually have friendly staff and customers.

The traditional snug areas are still a feature of many old pubs – closed-in

immortalised by Sean O'Casey.

The Crown Liquor Saloon in Great Victoria Street, Belfast, is the city's most flamboyant. It was built in 1885 by an architect who was inspired by what he had seen in Spain and

sections where a few friends can get together in relative privacy. There are plenty about. William Blake's, Church Street, in Enniskillen is one. In Dublin's Baggot Street Lower there's Doheny and Nesbitt's. Another is Kehoe's, in South Anne Street, Dublin, whose snugs were

Italy. The result is red and yellow ceilings, marble-topped bar with wooden arches and columns, and panelled snugs with ornate carvings over the doors. The pub is cared for by the National Trust, whose restoration work includes gas lamps (see page 98).

Some Irish pubs have a theme. Carmichael's of Holywood, Co Down, near the Belfast-Bangor railway, serves food and drink in what resembles railway carriages.

Music is a big attraction in many pubs – dozens of them in Dublin. Slattery's, in Capel Street, has traditional Irish music, rock and blues entertainment seven nights a week. Concerts are given at Bad Bob's Backstage Bar in Essex Street East, where traditional and folk, country and jazz are also played.

Many world-famous singers and bands started as pub musicians in Ireland.

Pubs are an institution in Ireland and an essential element of daily life. A visit is a pleasant way of getting to know the people

NIGHTCLUBS
BELFAST
Larry's Piano Bar
Lively atmosphere, '30s Bohemian-style extravagance, piano music.
36 Bedford Street. Tel: 028–9032 5061.

Live music at Larry's Piano Bar

Pips Nightclub
Located in a complex which includes Elbow's pub, a popular venue for live music.
Dublin Road. Tel: 028–9023 3003.

CO DONEGAL
Frankie's Niteclub
Tuesday teenagers' disco (no alcohol), disco nights Wednesday, Friday and Saturday, and Irish Country and Western bands on Saturday.
Meeting House Street, Raphoe.
Tel: 074–45153.

CO DUBLIN
Charlie's Rock Bar
One of Dublin's longest standing rock venues, the emphasis is still on live and loud.
2 Aungier Street, Dublin 2.
Tel: 01–475 5895.

CO LIMERICK
Baker Place
Pub/restaurant with late-night dancing.
Perry Square, Limerick. Tel: 061–418414.

CO LONDONDERRY
Squires Nightclub
Young people's rendezvous.
Shipquay Street, Londonderry.
Tel: 028–7126 6017.

PUB ENTERTAINMENT
BELFAST
The Front Page
Popular with local journalists. Live music Wednesday to Sunday.
108 Donegall Street, Belfast.
Tel: 028–9032 4924.
Kelly's Cellars
Saturday afternoon folk, Saturday night blues.
30 Bank Street, Belfast 1. Tel: 028–9032 4835.
Rotterdam Bar
Irish, folk, blues or jazz most nights.
54 Pilot Street, Belfast 1. Tel: 028–9074 6021.

CO CLARE
Archway
Restaurant/bar with great music.
Main Street, Ennistymon. Tel: 065–71080.

CO DONEGAL
Shamrock Lodge
Traditional Irish music, Wednesday and Saturday all year.
Falcarragh. Tel: 074–35192.

CO DUBLIN
International Bar
Lively venue for rock bands and other groups. Tuesday singer/songwriter night.
23 Wicklow Street, Dublin 2. Tel: 01–677 9250.

The Crown Liquor Saloon in Belfast is a fine example of a gaslit Victorian pub

Slattery's

Paul Brady performed here regularly 30 years ago. Still a top choice for rock, blues, trad and folk.
129 Capel Street, Dublin.
Tel: 01–872 7971.

CO LIMERICK
Nancy Blake's

Traditional music Sunday to Wednesday in one of the city's foremost bars.
Denmark Street, Limerick.
Tel: 061–416443.

CO LONDONDERRY
Dungloe Bar

One of the town's best pubs for music and quizzes.
Waterloo Street, Londonderry.
Tel: 028–7126 7716.
Townsman
Popular nightspot with young people.
33 Shipquay Street, Londonderry.
Tel: 028–7126 0820.

CO SLIGO
Knock na Shee Inn

Ballads, Irish music, singsongs.
Lavagh, Ballymote. Tel 071–84001.
Yeats Tavern
Music at weekends, traditional sessions in summer.
Drumcliff Bridge, Sligo. Tel: 071–63117.

THEATRES
BELFAST
Grand Opera House

Plays, opera, ballet and pantomime.
Great Victoria Street, Belfast 1.
Tel: 028–9024 1919.
Lyric Theatre
Drama based on Irish heritage.
Ridgeway Street, Belfast 7.
Tel: 028–9038 1081.

CO CORK
Cork Opera House

Variety, touring productions.
Lavitt's Quay, Cork. Tel: 021–270022.

CO DUBLIN
Abbey Theatre

Drama based on Irish culture.
Lower Abbey Street, Dublin 1.
Tel: 01– 878 7222.
Gate Theatre
Contemporary plays.
Cavendish Row, Parnell Square, Dublin 1.
Tel: 01–874 4045.
Olympia Theatre
Comedy, dance, drama – you name it.
Dame Street, Dublin 2. Tel: 01–677 7744.

CO KERRY
Siamsa Tíre National Folk Theatre

Summer music, folklore, song, dance.
Tralee. Tel: 066–23055.

MUSIC, MUSIC, MUSIC!

You know it when you hear it – you can't stop your feet tapping. Traditional Irish music is difficult to define, but easy to enjoy.

Although each new Irish generation promotes its own interpretation of traditional music, and adds to the range of ballads, there has been a swell in the trend in recent years.

Notes of political strife, emigration and rebellion against authority creep into ballads. Overtones of bawdiness and lust have never been away, and the sad solos of unrequited love, lost love and thwarted love continue to sell in mega-figures.

Irish singers and performers and Irish groups have worldwide impact. Music reverberates in the pubs and in the streets. Sometimes it is impromptu. Often it is 'all join in'.

The harp – the instrument most readily associated with Ireland – is seldom played as a traditional instrument today, though a musician playing one in Dublin's Grafton Street attracts huge crowds. The fiddle is at the hub of traditional Irish music.

The *uilleann* pipes, with the elbow used to pump air, are a refined version of bagpipes, and the *bodhran* – a small goatskin drum – is popular in West Cork and Kerry. It is beaten with the

In a pub, or out in the street, any time is a good time for music

Traditional music has a high profile
in Ireland

Irish harp maker, tuning a new instrument
at Marlay Park, Dublin

knuckles or a soft, double-ended
drumstick.

The tin whistle provides a merry
accompaniment to other instruments,
and the accordion and flute are often
played solo.

The Republic has a central
organisation for promoting music, song
and dance – the Comhaltas. Its annual
booklet, a guide to traditional music
organised by Comhaltas branches
nationwide, is available free from
tourist information centres.

At the end of August the three-day
All-Ireland Fleadh (pronounced *flah*),
held in a different location each year,
marks the highlight of the traditional
music calendar.

Festivals and Events

*F*estivals large and small are staged throughout Ireland to celebrate activities, interests and anniversaries ranging from the cultural to the practical, from the commonplace to the bizarre. Whatever the event – whether it is concerned with horses or roses, art or oysters – it will almost certainly involve music, often traditional, and it will definitely be fun.

Here is a month-by-month round-up of some of the major events staged annually in both the Republic and Northern Ireland. Some are held in a different location each year, and dates may drift into the previous or succeeding month. Tourist offices will have up-to-date information.

January
The Royal Dublin Society's Irish Crafts Fair, Dublin; major horse races at Gowran Park (Co Kilkenny), Leopardstown (Co Dublin), Naas (Co Kildare) and Thurles (Co Tipperary).

February
International Arts Festival, Dublin; Goffs bloodstock sales, Kill, Co Kildare; Ulster Motor Show, Belfast.

March
Belfast Musical Festival; Heavy Horse Show and ploughing match, Ballycastle, Co Antrim; St Patrick's Day (17 March) celebrations throughout Ireland – big parades in Belfast and Dublin; pilgrimages at Cultra, Downpatrick and Newry, all in Co Down; Jameson Ulster National steeplechase, Downpatrick, Co Down.

April
Arklow Music Festival, Co Wicklow; Belfast Civic Festival and Lord Mayor's Show; Dublin Film Festival, Dublin; Dublin International Piano Competition; Jameson Irish Grand National, Fairyhouse, Co Meath; Pan Celtic International Festival, Tralee, Co Kerry; World (Irish) Dancing Championships, Republic.

May
Murphy's International Mussel Fair, Bantry, Co Cork; Cork International Choral Festival; Dundalk International Maytime Festival, Co Louth; Fermanagh Lakelands Fishing Festival; Fleadh Ceoil (traditional music, song and dance), Republic; Royal Ulster Agricultural Society Show, Belfast; Spring Show and Industries Fair, Dublin.

June
Budweiser Irish Derby, The Curragh, Co Kildare; Bloomsday (16 June), celebration of James Joyce's *Ulysses*, Dublin; Dun Laoghaire Festival, Co Dublin; Feis na nGleann (music, dancing, sport), Ballycastle, Co Antrim; AIB Music Festival in Great Irish Houses, all Ireland; Fiddle Stone Festival – Irish fiddlers gather at Belleek, Co Fermanagh; Listowel Writers' Week Listowel, Co Kerry; Lough Swilly International Tope Festival, Rathmullen, Co Donegal.

July
Bray Seaside Festival, Co Wicklow; Cork International Folk Dance Festival; Galway Arts Festival; Galway Races; King of Dalkey Festival, Co Dublin; City of Belfast International Rose Trials; Medieval Fair, Carrickfergus, Co Antrim;

Battle of the Boyne Commemoration (Orangemen's Day – 12 July), Northern Ireland; Skibbereen Welcome Festival, Co Cork; Ulster Harp Derby, Co Down.

August

Ancient Order of Hibernians' Parade (15 August, Feast of the Assumption), Co Londonderry; Clifden Pony Show, Co Galway; Dublin Horse Show; Kilkenny Arts Week; Mary from Dungloe International Festival,

Autumn Season, Grand Opera House, Belfast; Waterford International Festival of Light Opera.

October

Ballinasloe International Horse Fair and Festival – one of Europe's largest horse fairs, Co Galway; Cork International Film and Jazz Festivals; Dublin City Marathon; Kinsale International Gourmet Festival, Co Cork; Sligo Arts Festival; Wexford Festival of Opera.

Dixon Park is host to the City of Belfast's International Rose Trials every July

Dunglow, Co Donegal; O'Carolan Harp and Traditional Music Festival, Boyle, Co Roscommon; Oul' Lammas Fair, Ballycastle, Co Antrim; Puck Fair, Killorglin, Co Kerry; Relief of Derry Celebrations commemorating siege of 1688–9; Rose of Tralee International Festival, Co Kerry; Skibbereen Horse Fair, Co Cork.

September

Belfast Folk Festival; Clarenbridge Oyster Festival, Co Galway; Dublin Flower Show; Matchmaking Festival – the ultimate singles party, Lisdoonvarna, Co Clare; Opera Northern Ireland

November

Belfast Festival – a cornucopia of music, from classical to jazz, as well as drama, opera and cinema in and around Queen's University; Bard of Armagh Festival, Keady, Co Armagh.

December

Christmas horse-racing, Leopardstown, Co Dublin; New Year Viennese Ball, Belfast City Hall; Wren Boys Festival, Bunratty Folk Park, Co Clare. Wren Boys in fancy dress and with blackened faces traditionally sing and dance in the streets and demand money (for charity nowadays).

Children

AMUSEMENT CENTRES

Children of any age will enjoy a visit to one of the amusement parks, where attractions range from slides and pools to rides and arcades.

Leisureland Amusement Park

Wide selection of rides, waterslides and heated indoor pool.

Salthill, Galway.

Mack's Amusements

Videos, slot machines, children's rides, bingo. Open 10am–midnight.

Main Street, Bundoran, Co Donegal.

Tramore Amusement Park

Many rides and attractions. Tramore seafront also has a miniature railway.

Seafront, Tramore, Co Waterford.

Tropicana

Slides, adventure playground, variety shows, drama, films.

Central Promenade, Newcastle, Co Down.

Waterworld

An indoor complex with an 80m water flume, whirlpools, entertainment with water cannon and pirate ship and relaxing saunas and jacuzzis to provide a contrast. Also under cover is a funfair.

Portrush, Co Antrim.

BEACHES

Given good weather – and that is something that cannot be taken for granted in Ireland – many children are happy to spend time paddling in the sea and building sandcastles on the lovely and often uncrowded beaches. But the time comes when they want a little more adventure and excitement.

The vast majority of Irish beaches – they call them strands – remain delightfully natural. But in the shadow of the Binevenagh Mountain at Lough Foyle, Co Londonderry, lie 5km of clean sand, the Strand of Benone, and adjacent to it is the **Benone Tourist Complex**. Here smaller children can splash about under supervision in heated pools, while older ones can enjoy the thrills of the adventure playground.

Portrush has generous lengths of sandy beach, with donkey rides and candy floss.

The busy seaside resort of Bundoran, Co Donegal, has its own Waterworld, an indoor heated **Aqua Adventure Playground** on the seafront. It has a wave pool and a slide for small children,

The traditional seaside resort of Newcastle

as well as a choice of long, short, fast, slow, straight or spiral slides.

Tramore, Co Waterford, has a wide sweep of beach, a miniature railway and an amusement park.

BOAT TRIPS/WATER SPORTS

Most children love a boat trip. In Glengarriff, Co Cork, boatmen vie for the privilege of transporting summer visitors – at a negotiable fee – to **Garinish Island** in Bantry Bay, a 10- to 15-minute ride away. Seals are often seen swimming, or basking on rocks. Italian gardens, including subtropical plants, are the big attraction on the island. Children can explore woodland paths, a Grecian-style temple and a Martello tower (see page 70).

Another interesting boat cruise goes past the wooded islands of **Killarney's Lower Lake**.

You can hire rowing boats or canoes in many towns and villages situated on rivers, canals or lakes.

Sea canoeing is an option at a few centres. At **Marble Hill Strand**, 6km east of Dunfanaghy, Co Donegal, children over 10 can receive instruction and go on a supervised expedition. Windsurfing is also taught. Wetsuits and equipment can be hired.

CAVES

Caves are always fascinating. Among the most dramatic are **Marble Arch Caves,** near Blacklion, Co Fermanagh – part of the tour is by electric boat (see page 110) – and **Aillwee Cave,** Ballyvaughan, Co Clare, inhabited long ago by brown bears (see page 75).

HORSE-RIDING

Ireland has residential riding centres where instruction is given, or where trail riding is offered. There are also non-residential centres which take novices, including children, for basic instruction by the hour.

MUSEUMS

Many of the exhibits at Belfast's **Ulster Folk and Transport Museum** appeal to children, and on Saturdays in summer a miniature railway operates (see page 103).

Belfast Zoo

ZOOS AND WILDLIFE

Belfast Zoo is situated on Cave Hill – the higher you go the steeper it gets (see page 96). Dublin Zoo, in Phoenix Park opened more than 160 years ago (see page 27).

The Ark Open Zoo in Newtownards gives visitors the chance to see over 80 rare breeds of animal including cattle, pigs, sheep, goats, ponies, ducks, poultry and llamas (see page 100).

Westport House, Westport, Co Mayo, has a zoo and a wonderfully equipped children's playground (see page 84). Visitors can observe the milking routine from a gallery, see animals and poultry and also follow a nature trail at **Streamvale.** This is Northern Ireland's first open dairy farm, and is located at Ballyhanwood Road, Dundonald, Belfast.

Sport

SPECTATOR SPORTS

Ireland generally manages to maintain a reasonably high profile in international sports – especially rugby and soccer – but traditional games continue to attract a huge following. The most striking characteristics of traditional games are the fervour and sportsmanship of the players and the exemplary behaviour of the fans. The All-Ireland finals of the Gaelic Games inter-county championships are played in September, usually at Croke Park, Dublin.

BULLETS

The strangest sport – and from the spectator's point of view, potentially most dangerous – is bullets, or road bowls, which entails throwing a metal ball weighing almost 1kg over a course covering several kilometres of winding public roads. People say the game was originally played with cannonballs. Once played throughout Ireland, bullets is mostly confined to the lanes of Counties Armagh and Cork, but it is also played in many small towns and villages. Some tournaments attract teams from Gaelic communities abroad.

GAELIC FOOTBALL

Gaelic football, a hybrid of soccer and rugby, is played with a round ball and involves two 15-strong teams whose members may handle the ball.

HORSE-RACING

Ireland has 27 courses, offering racing over 250 days of the year. Sunday racing has been introduced in recent years, and evening meetings are held from May to August. The headquarters of Irish racing is the Curragh, Co Kildare, where the Budweiser Irish Derby is run in June. Another classic, the Kildangan Stud Irish Oaks, is held at the Curragh in July.

The Jameson Irish Grand National event takes place at Fairyhouse, Co Meath, at Easter. Other National Hunt courses are at Galway, Gowran Park, Navan and Punchestown.

Festival meetings which combine National Hunt and Flat Racing, are held at Galway, Gowran Park, Killarney, Listowel, Tralee and Tramore. The Irish Point-to-Point season of rural steeple chases runs from January to May. Events are staged every Sunday.

A calendar giving full details of racing is available from the Irish Horse-Racing Authority, Leopardstown Racecourse, Foxrock, Dublin 18 (tel: 01–289 7277).

In Northern Ireland the major event is the Jameson Ulster National steeple chase, staged in March at Downpatrick.

The Irish National Stud and the Irish Horse Museum are both at Tully, Co Kildare (tel: 045–521617). The museum tells the story of the Irish horse from prehistoric times. Its centrepiece is the skeleton of the famous racehorse, Arkle.

HURLING

The national game is hurling. An ancient game – it is mentioned in early Irish legends – hurling looks like a cross between rugby, hockey, lacrosse and guerrilla warfare. Played between teams of 15 burly men (there is a women's version, called camogie), it is said to be the world's fastest field game. The players belt a small leather ball with hockey-like sticks. The ball may be caught but not thrown. Hurling fields, found all over the Republic and in some parts of Northern Ireland, look like rugby pitches except that goalposts are netted below the crossbar.

RUGBY

Local matches are played at weekends throughout the Republic and Northern Ireland. In Dublin, international matches take place at the Lansdowne Road stadium. Details of fixtures can be found in the national and local press.

Racing is hugely popular in Ireland and a major social event

SHOWJUMPING

Showjumping is one of Ireland's main weekend attractions, with more than 500 events taking place each year, some held in conjunction with agricultural shows. Country shows offer an attractive spectacle and provide an insight into Irish rural life. A full list of shows is available from the Showjumping Association of Ireland, Anglesea Lodge, Anglesea Road, Ballsbridge, Dublin 4 (tel: 01–660 1700).

SKITTLES

Another traditional game now being revived in Ulster is crossroads skittles. Popular before the advent of television in Cavan, Donegal, Fermanagh, Leitrim and Monaghan, the game is re-emerging at fairs and festivals, and championships have been staged in Co Fermanagh.

PARTICIPATORY SPORTS

Fresh air and fitness are easy to find in Ireland, where the opportunities for outdoor pursuits are many and varied. Indoor facilities – swimming pools and gymnasia – are found in many luxury and resort hotels.

EQUESTRIAN SPORTS

Ireland and the horse are synonymous, and there are riding centres, residential and non-residential, everywhere you go. Even those visitors staying in Dublin or Belfast will not have far to travel to get into the saddle.

Among some 20 or so different establishments in the Dublin area are the Carrickmines Equestrian Centre, Glenamuck Road, Foxrock, Dublin 18

(tel: 01–295 5990) and Brooke Lodge Riding Centre, Burrow Road, Stepaside (tel: 01–295 2153).

Belfast's closest riding establishment is the year-round Lagan Valley Equestrian Centre, Dunmurry (tel: 028–9061 4853).

Trail-riding, where overnight accommodation is provided in farmhouses, country homes and hotels, or at stay-put centres, is available in many rural areas.

Arrangements can also be made for

visitors to participate in hunting. More detailed information on riding holidays can be obtained from any Irish Tourist Board or Northern Ireland Tourist Board office, or from the Association of Irish Riding Establishments, 11 Moore Park, Newbridge, Co Kildare (tel: 045–431584).

Ireland's sporting facilities are second to none

GOLF

There are over 350 golf courses in Ireland that welcome visitors. Those in the Dublin area include the Royal Dublin Golf Club, North Bull Island, Dollymount (tel: 01–833 6346) and the Arnold Palmer-designed course at the Kildare Hotel and Country Club, Straffan, Co Kildare (tel: 01–601 7200). Belfast has about a dozen clubs within 8km of the city centre. Information is available from the Golfing Union of Ireland, 81 Eglinton Road, Dublin 4 (tel: 01–269 4111).

SAILING

Ireland's varied coastline – to say nothing of its many lakes – offers everything from windsurfing and dinghy-sailing to sedate cruising and rugged ocean racing.

The most popular cruising area, between Cork Harbour and the Dingle Peninsula, offers 143 totally different places where a boat can moor safely and peacefully for an overnight stay. Harbours like Youghal, Dunmore East and Kinsale extend a welcome to yachtsmen in their friendly bars and restaurants.

Sailing schools are located at a number of places on the Irish Sea and Atlantic coasts. For information contact the Irish Sailing Association, 3 Park Road, Dun Laoghaire, Co Dublin (tel: 01– 280 0239).

The Irish Tourist Board issues a leaflet with details of yacht charter companies. In Northern Ireland, the Fermanagh Tourist Information Centre, Wellington Road, Enniskillen, Co Fermanagh, (tel: 028–6632 3110) has information on watersports facilities on Lough Erne.

TENNIS

Although the Irish climate is often unsympathetic, tennis is growing in popularity. Public courts can be found in the cities and larger towns, and about 100 hotels have grass or hard courts.

Dublin is well served, with public facilities at Bushy Park (tel: 01–490 0320), Herbert Park (tel: 01–668 4364) and St Anne's Park (tel: 01–831 3697).

For further information contact Tennis Ireland, Argyle Square, Donnybrook, Dublin 4 (tel: 01–668 1841).

FISHING

Few countries offer such a profusion of well-stocked fishing waters as Ireland, and few market their angling facilities so expertly or so affordably. Festivals and competitions in coarse, game and sea angling are open for visitors. Sea angling and coarse fishing are year-round activities in Ireland.

For fishing in private water, the permission of the owner must be obtained. A licence may be required for game fishing, but licences are not needed for sea fishing.

In the Republic be sure to stay at accommodation registered with and approved by Bord Fáilte. Specialist accommodation offers such amenities as meals served to suit ideal local fishing times, copious hot water, a rod room and overnight clothes drying. Your gamefish catch can be deep frozen or smoked to take home.

For the *Angling in Ireland* guide, listing approved accommodation, write to Bord Fáilte (Irish Tourist Board), Baggot Street Bridge, Dublin 2 (tel: 01–602 4000).

The Northern Ireland Tourist Board publishes *Where to Stay in Northern Ireland,* listing a range of accommodation. The book may be ordered with a cheque or postal order for £4.99 sterling or equivalent from the Tourist Information Office, Northern Ireland Tourist Board, St Anne's Court, 59 North Street, Belfast BT1 1NB (tel: 028–9023 1221), or from bookshops. The NITB also issues free Information Bulletins on sea fishing from boats (No 9), fishing from the seashore (No 10), game fishing (No 23) and coarse fishing (No 28).

For the addresses of overseas offices of both boards see page 189.

For the latest information on licensing and permits contact the appropriate Angling Federation listed below.

ADDRESSES

National Coarse Fishing Federation of Ireland
'Blaithín', Dublin Road, Cavan (tel: 049–32367).
Irish Federation of Sea Anglers
67 Windsor Drive, Monkstown, Co Dublin (tel: 01–280 6873).
Trout Anglers Federation of Ireland
Headford, Co Galway (tel: 093–35494).

ADVENTURE PURSUITS

Mountains in Ireland are mostly well-rounded ranges rather than high jagged peaks, which means an absence of vicious air currents.

Add the facts that most of the hills are free of trees, power lines and other encumbrances and that many of them provide a soft landing on peat, and it is clear that Ireland has near-ideal conditions for gliding and hang-gliding. On good days pilots can enjoy soaring for hours at a time. There are guided tours between March and September and tuition is available.

Parachuting, which for the dedicated enthusiast can lead to skydiving, takes place at weekends in Ireland's two centres. A first-timer can jump from an aircraft after a day's training.

Few hills and mountains of Ireland exceed 920m but they provide interesting climbs, beauty and solitude. Mountain rescue teams with helicopter back-up operate in the main areas.

Ballina stands at the mouth of the Moy, one of the country's best salmon rivers

Because there are few tracks, maps and compasses should always be carried.

Canoeing is one of Ireland's fastest-growing sports, on coastal and inland waters. It takes place all year. As well as touring and camping by canoe – the option of most visitors – there are summer marathons, flat-water sprints and, for the highly skilled, surfing.

White-water racing – timed runs over very rough stretches of river – and slaloms are other exciting aspects of canoeing.

ADDRESSES
Association For Adventure Sports
House of Sport, Long Mile Road, Walkinstown, Dublin 12, comprises:
Irish Hang Gliding Association
(tel: 01–450 9845);
Mountaineering Council of Ireland
(tel: 01–450 9845);
Irish Canoe Union (tel: 01–450 9838).

Parachute Association of Ireland
116 Oliver Plunkett Road, Dun Laoghaire, Co Dublin
(tel: 01–873 0093).

Food and Drink

*P*laces to eat out in the Republic and Northern Ireland vary from coffee shops and pubs to high-class restaurants and the occasional castle offering medieval-style dining. Generally, prices are lower in the North. It is wise to book in advance or arrive early for anything but the most casual of evening meals – this applies particularly on Sundays in the North where some places are closed. Some restaurants, including those in hotels in both North and South, serve food nearly all day – luncheons, snacks and high tea – then close their dining room at 7 or 8pm. Except in the fashionable parts of major cities, people tend to eat early.

Expect to pay around £2 for a pint of Guinness – other stouts may be cheaper. Some unlicensed premises don't mind you bringing your own wine.

The £ symbol is used as an approximate guide to the price bracket of each place listed – for a three-course meal per person, excluding wine or coffee. In the Republic the symbol represents the punt. Service charges, if they exist, vary, so check the menu.

£ = under £10
££ = £10–£15
£££ = £15–£20
££££ = over £20

LEINSTER
DUBLIN CENTRAL
Ante Room Seafood Restaurant ££
Also vegetarian, Irish beef and lamb.
20 Lower Baggot Street, Temple Bar,
Dublin 2. Tel: 01–661 8832.

Bad Ass Cafe £
The pizzeria for fun and noise – video, juke box, music. Demijohns of wine.
9–11 Crown Alley, Temple Bar, Dublin 2.
Tel: 01–671 2596.

Bewley's Oriental Café £
One of four locations of this popular café/restaurant, the main one in Grafton Street. Eclectic mix of food and people.
Grafton Street, Dublin 2. Tel: 01–677 6761.

Brokers Restaurant ££
Fully licensed Irish family restaurant. Traditional food and vegetarian.
25 Dame Street, Dublin 2.
Tel: 01–679 3534.

Le Caprice ££££
Italian/continental. Pastas, veal, vegetarian.
12 St Andrew's Street, Dublin 2.
Tel: 01–679 4050. Closed Monday.

The Cedar Tree ££
Lebanese cuisine and vegetarian dishes in Arabian-style 'cavern'.
11a St Andrew's Street, Dublin 2.
Tel: 01–677 2121.

Chapter One £££
Irish and continental cuisine, vegetarian. Basement of Dublin Writers Museum.
18–19 Parnell Square North, Dublin 2.
Tel: 01–873 2266. Closed Sunday,
Monday and lunch Saturday.

The Commons Restaurant ££££
Classic international food.
Newman House, 85–6 St Stephen's Green,
Dublin 2. Tel: 01–478 0530. Closed:
Sunday and lunch Saturday.

Dillon's Restaurant ££
Irish stew, steaks, fish, vegetarian.
21 Suffolk Street, Dublin 2.
Tel: 01–677 4804.

No 27 – The Green ££££
Modern Irish cuisine in historic hotel.

The Shelbourne Hotel, 27 St Stephen's Green, Dublin 2. Tel: 01–676 2727.

Old Dublin Restaurant ££££
Russian and Scandinavian cuisine, fish a speciality.
91 Francis Street, Dublin 8. Tel: 01–454 2028/454 2346. Closed: Sunday.

Polo's ££££
Go for the décor and modern artwork as well as the Californian/Continental fare.
Schoolhouse Lane, off Molesworth Street, Dublin 2. Tel: 01–676 6442/676 3362. Closed: Sunday.

Tosca £
Pasta, pizza, casual Italian eating all day till late.
20 Suffolk Street, Dublin 2. Tel: 01–679 6744.

DUBLIN SOUTH

Chandni's Restaurant ££
Noted Tandoori food accompanied by sitar music.
174 Pembroke Road, Ballsbridge, Dublin 4. Tel: 01–668 9088. Closed: Sunday lunchtime.

Ernie's ££££
Designed around a mulberry tree. Many Irish paintings displayed. Charcoal grills, game in season.
Mulberry Gardens, Donnybrook, Dublin 4. Tel: 01–269 3300/269 3260. Closed Sunday and Monday.

**Jurys Hotel and Towers
(The Coffee Dock) ££**
Top-grade hotel with three restaurants, as well as this coffee shop.
Ballsbridge, Dublin 4. Tel: 01–660 5000. Open: 6am–5am the next day, closes 11pm Sunday and opens 7am Monday.

Kitty O'Shea's ££
Spacious 200-seat restaurant of the Parnell era – late 19th-century.
23–5 Upper Grand Canal Street, Dublin 4. Tel: 01–660 9965/660 8050.

Locks £££
Small French provincial-style restaurant by Grand Canal. Classical and modern cuisine.
1 Windsor Terrace, Portobello, Dublin 8. Tel: 01–454 3391. Closed: Saturday lunchtime and Sunday.

Sachs £££
Small, Georgian-style restaurant serving fish, steaks, poultry, vegetarian and gluten-free dishes.
Donnybrook, Dublin 4. Tel: 01– 668 0995.

Good solid fare – Irish stew is traditionally made with lamb

Ireland is renowned for its excellent salmon and variety of seafood

DUBLIN NORTH
Brahms & Liszt ££
Family restaurant near Dublin Airport. Extensive choice of food, competitively priced.
Swords Road, Santry, Dublin 9.
Tel: 01–842 8383.

CO CARLOW
The Lord Bagnel Inn ££
Good food in pleasant atmosphere.
Leighlinbridge. Tel: 0503–21668.

CO DUBLIN
Abbey Tavern ££££
Turf fires, original stone walls, flagged floors and gaslights. Fish a speciality.
Abbey Street, Howth, Dublin 13.
Tel: 01–839 0307. Closed: Sunday.
Ayumi-Ya Japanese Restaurant £££
Japanese cuisine. Teppan-Yaki, sushi, vegetarian.
Newpark Centre, Newtownpark Avenue, Blackrock. Tel: 01–283 1767. Closed Sunday lunch.
Beaufield Mews ££
Good value fish and game dishes. Inexpensive wines.
Woodlands Avenue, Stillorgan.

Tel: 01–288 0375.
Dinner only, except Sunday lunch.
Bon Appetit ££££
Fresh seafood, veal, steaks, duck. Also vegetarian and gluten-free dishes.
9 James Terrace, Malahide.
Tel: 01–845 0314. Closed: Saturday lunch and Sunday.
Cooper's Wine Bar ££
Indian, Chinese and European food in converted 18th-century premises.
8 The Crescent, Monkstown.
Tel: 01–284 2037/284 2995.
De Selby's ££
Reasonable prices and personality. Vegetarian and gluten-free dishes.
17–18 Patrick Street, Dun Laoghaire.
Tel: 01–284 1761/2.
Giovanni's ££
Informal Italian restaurant serving pasta, pizzas, steaks and fish.
3–4 Townyard Lane, Malahide.
Tel: 01–845 1733.
Healy's Black Lion Inn ££
Founded in 1838, the inn specialises in steaks and seafood.
Orchard Road, Main Street, Clondalkin, Dublin 22. Tel: 01–457 4814/457 4253.
Open: noon–11.30pm (10.30pm on Sunday).

Howth Lodge Hotel Restaurant £££
AA 3-star family-run hotel serving
charcoal-grilled fresh fish and steaks.
Howth. Tel: 01–832 1010.
**Redbank Guesthouse and
Restaurant ££££**
Chef/proprietor cooks catch of the day,
landed at the pier each evening.
*6–7 Church Street, Skerries. Tel: 01–849
1005. Closed: Sunday dinner and Monday.*

CO KILDARE
Red House Inn £££
Haute cuisine; home-grown vegetables.
Turf fires.
*Newbridge. Tel: 045–31516/31657.
Closed: Sunday and Monday.*
Springfield Hotel £££
Family-run hotel. Restaurant offers a
variety of Vegetarian dishes.
*Leixlip. Tel: 01–624 49265.
Open: 12.30pm–11.30pm.*

CO KILKENNY
**Mount Juliet Estate (Lady Helen
McCalmont Restaurant) ££££**
Fine linen, crystal and silverware reflects
quality cuisine.
Thomastown. Tel: 056–24455.
Parliament House £££
Victorian ambience. Vegetarian and
gluten-free dishes available.
*24–5 Parliament Street, Kilkenny.
Tel: 056–63666.*

CO WESTMEATH
The Castle Pantry ££
Quality home-cooking in a 600-year-old
castle. Vegetarian dishes.
Tyrrellspass Castle. Tel: 044–23105.
Jolly Mariner ££
Large, pleasant restaurant beside the
River Shannon. Vegetarian choices.
*Abbey Road, Athlone. Tel: 0902–721113.
Closed: Monday, Tuesday (open summer).*

CO WEXFORD
The Bohemian Girl ££
The owner/chef prepares meat and
seafood and has been a frequent award
winner.
*North Main Street, Wexford.
Tel: 053–24419.*
Hotel Rosslare £££
Award-winning bar food. Restaurant
handy for ferryboat passengers.
*Opposite Rosslare Harbour.
Tel: 053–33110.*

CO WICKLOW
Pizza del Forno ££
Restaurant/steakhouse/pizzeria.
*The Mall Centre, Main Street, Wicklow.
Tel: 0404–67075.*
Tree of Idleness ££££
International gourmet dishes, including
Greek. Award-winning wine list.
*Seafront, Bray. Tel: 01–286 3498/
282 8183. Closed: Monday.*

MUNSTER
CO CLARE
Auburn Lodge Hotel ££
Irish and international food; vegetarian
dishes.
Galway Road, Ennis. Tel: 065–6821247.
Bali Room Restaurant £££
Indonesian and Irish fare in small
friendly restaurant.
*Weaver Inn, Newmarket-on-Fergus.
Tel: 061–368114. Closed: Sunday.*
Crotty's £
This combined pub/guesthouse is noted
for excellent simple fare and legendary
traditional music sessions.
Kilrush. Tel: 065–9052470
Dromoland Castle ££££
Impressive chandeliers and candles
enhance the setting for a romantic
evening.
Newmarket-on-Fergus. Tel: 061–368144.

CO CORK

Barn Restaurant £££
Fresh Irish produce, distinctive cuisine.
Lotamore, Glanmire. Tel: 021–866211.

Bistro Seafood Winebar £££
Specialising in fresh local produce.
Guardwell, Kinsale. Tel: 021–774193.
Closed: Monday to Saturday lunchtime.

Blarney Park Hotel
(Clancarthy Restaurant) ££
Wholesome food in relaxed surroundings.
Blarney. Tel: 021–385281.

Casey's Cabin ££
Go for the view and the seafood.
Baltimore. Tel: 028–20197. Closes: 9pm.
Also closed Sunday 2–5pm.

Castle Hotel ££
Family-run hotel which has won awards
for its tourist menu.
Macroom. Tel: 026–41074. Closes: 8.30pm.

Dun-Mhuire Restaurant ££
Fish a speciality. Vegetarian available.
Kilbarry Road, Dunmanway. Tel: 023–
45162. Closed: Sunday to Tuesday.

Doloree House £££
Continental finesse to fresh local
produce. Vegetarian, gluten-free dishes.
Lisavaird, Clonakilty. Tel: 023–34123.
Closed: Monday (except Bank Holidays).

Finins £££
Quality food, bar menu.
75 Main Street, Midleton.
Tel: 021–631878/632382. Closed: Sunday.

Flemings £££
Modern French-Irish cuisine in
Georgian country house surroundings.
Silver Grange House, Tivoll, Cork.
Tel: 021–821621/821178.

John Barleycorn Inn £££
Steaks, fresh fish. Vegetarian and gluten-
free dishes.
Riverstown, Glanmire. Tel: 021–821499.

Tung Sing ££
Chinese restaurant on Cork's main
thoroughfare.
23a Patrick Street, Cork.
Tel: 021– 274616.

Vickery's Inn £££
Varied menus while bar food is served
all day.
New Street, Bantry. Tel: 027–50006.

Victoria Hotel ££
Vegetarian meals on menu.
Macroom. Tel: 026–41082.

Westlodge Hotel £££
Seafood a speciality. Children are well
catered for.
Bantry. Tel: 027–50360.

GOURMET CAPITAL

Kinsale is the haunt of epicures from around the world early in October when this fishing port holds a four-day International Gourmet Festival. Throughout the year the ancient town attracts discerning diners, having firmly established itself as Ireland's Gourmet Capital.

In 1975, 12 restaurants got together to form the Kinsale Good Food Circle, and excellent seafood is served at all of them. Vegetarians can always find something tasty and unusual, like the nettle soup and courgette and herb bake at the Cottage Loft, Main Street. Locally picked wild spinach and locally farmed mussels are featured on the menu at the Blue Haven, on the site of the old fishmarket. Walnut soup is an interesting starter at The Captain's Table in Acton's Hotel, and a memorable monkfish in tarragon sauce and white wine is served at Max's Wine Bar, in Main Street.

Windmill Tavern £££
Seafood and gourmet cooking.
46 North Street, Skibbereen. Tel: 028–
21606. Closed: Sunday in winter.

CO KERRY
Arbutus Hotel (Pat's Restaurant) £
Fresh, home-made meals.
College Street, Killarney. Tel: 064–31037.
Beginish Restaurant £££
Emphasis on seafood.
Green Street, Dingle. Tel 066–9151588.
Closed: Monday.
Chez Jean-Marc £££
Imaginative French cuisine.
29 Castle Street, Tralee. Tel:
066–7121377. Closed: Sunday.
Eviston House Hotel
(Colleen Bawn Restaurant) £££
Fine food in elegant surroundings.
New Street, Killarney. Tel: 064–31640.
College Street, Killarney. Tel: 064–33404.
Kiely's Restaurant ££
Very extensive dinner and à la carte.
College Street, Killarney. Tel: 064–31656.
Mickey Neds £
Home-made dishes and delicatessen fare
in a friendly atmosphere.
Henry Street, Kenmare. Tel: 064–41591.
The Three Mermaids £££
Award-winning pub/restaurant.
William Street, Listowel.
Tel: 068–21184/22443.

CO LIMERICK
The Castle Oaks Hotel £££
Georgian-style dining room.
Castleconnell. Tel: 061–377666.
Mustard Seed £££
Over 100 dishes offered in village house
with original Irish kitchen.
Adare. Tel: 061–396451. Closed: Sunday,
Monday, and all of February.
Patrick Punches ££
Roasts, prime steaks, seafood.

Punches Cross, Limerick. Tel: 061–229588.
Shangrila ££
Peking and Cantonese dishes.
103 O'Connell Street, Limerick.
Tel: 061–414177.

CO TIPPERARY
Buttermarket Restaurant
'La Scala' ££
Friendly, family-run restaurant.
Vegetarian dishes.
Market Street, Clonmel. Tel: 052–24147.
Closed: Sunday evening.
The Fox's Den £££
Cellar-like restaurant with character.
Modreeny, Cloughjordan. Tel: 0505–
42210 (after 2.30pm). Closed: Sunday,
and Monday evenings.

CO WATERFORD
Dwyers of Mary Street ££
Quiet little restaurant with short but
impact-making menu.
8 Mary Street, Waterford.
Tel: 051–27478/21183. Closed: Sunday.
Merry's ££
Seafood restaurant in 17th-century wine
merchant's store. Bar food all day.
Lower Main Street, Dungarvan.
Tel: 058–41974/42818.
The Ship £££
Extensive menu includes seafood,
vegetarian.
Dunmore East, Waterford.
Tel: 051–83141/83144.
Waterford Castle £££
Chef Paul McCloskey uses local organic
produce.
The Island, Ballinakill. Tel: 051–78203.
The Wine Vault £–££
Good value lunch and evening meals are
served in this friendly bistro, situated in
the oldest part of the city. Good
selection of wines.
High Street, Waterford. Tel: 051–853444.

CONNACHT

CO GALWAY

Boluisce Cottage Bar ££

Award-winning seafood bar and restaurant. Vegetarian dishes.
Spiddall Village, Connemara. Tel: 091–83286.

Connemara Coast Hotel (The Gallery) £££

Views over Galway Bay, original paintings displayed. Live piano music.
Furbo. Tel: 091–92108.

Dun Aonghusa ££

Restaurant overlooking Galway Bay.
Kilronan, Inishmore, Aran Islands. Tel: 099–61104.

Galleon Restaurant £

Reputation for good Irish stew, fish and steaks at budget prices.
Salthill, Galway. Tel: 091–521266/522963. Open: to midnight.

Glynsk House £££

Lobster, salmon, oysters, mussels, shrimps and other seafood.
Carna Road, Cashel, Connemara. Tel: 095–32279.

Lydon's ££

Family restaurant. Children welcome.
5 Shop Street, Galway. Tel: 091–564051/566586.

Meadow Court Restaurant/Bar £££

Multi award-winning establishment specialising in fresh seafood and extensive international cuisine.
Loughrea. Tel: 091–841051/841633.

Owenmore Restaurant ££

Country house restaurant serving fresh home-made dishes; local seafood a speciality.
Ballynahinch Castle, Recess, Connemara. Tel: 095–31006. Closed: February.

Paddy Burkes £££

Connoisseurs from around the world experience the Clarenbridge oyster here. Steaks and seafood.
The Oyster Inn, Clarenbridge. Tel: 091–796226.

Peacocks ££

Fresh fish and quality steaks competitively priced.
Maam Cross. Tel: 091–82306.

CO MAYO

The Moorings ££

Cordon bleu cooking, fresh local ingredients in family restaurant.
The Quay, Westport. Tel: 098–25874. Closed: Sunday.

Swiss Barn Speciality Restaurant £££

Small, highly rated restaurant offering fondues, lobster thermidor, home-made ice creams.
Foxford Road, Ballina. Tel: 096–21117. Closed: Monday (except Bank Holidays).

CO SLIGO

Dragon House Restaurant ££

Cantonese, seafood, vegetarian dishes.
17 Temple Street, Sligo. Tel: 071–44688/44696.

ULSTER

BELFAST CENTRAL

Fat Harry's £

Steaks, grills.
91 Castle Street, Belfast 1. Tel: 028–9023 2226. Open: in the evening to 9pm.

Front Page £

Prawns in garlic and haddock mornay are among specials. Vegetarian dishes.
106 Donegall Street, Belfast 1. Tel: 028–9032 4269. Open: Monday to Saturday noon–9.30pm.

Nick's Warehouse ££

Try warm salad of pigeon breast with balsamic dressing, or smoked salmon mousse with smoked salmon as a starter. Imaginative vegetarian food.
35–9 Hill Street, Belfast 1. Tel: 028–9043 9690. Closed: Saturday and Sunday.

BELFAST – GOLDEN MILE

Arthur's ££
Try seafood mousse profiteroles or pork escalope with Stilton and raspberry sauce.
7 Hope Street, Belfast 2. Tel: 028–9033 3311. Closed: Sunday.

Bananas ££
Good continental and oriental food.
4 Clarence Street, Belfast 2. Tel: 028–9033 9999. Closed: Sunday.

La Belle Epoque £££
French cuisine, game in season.
61 Dublin Road, Belfast 2. Tel: 028– 9032 3244.

Café Orleans £
Pasta, steaks and seafood.
34 Bedford Street, Belfast 2. Tel: 028–9032 5061. Closed: Sunday and Monday.

Charmers ££
Try the stuffed mushrooms or pavlova.
85 Dublin Road, Belfast 2. Tel: 028–9023 8787. Closed: Sunday.

China Town £
Good Cantonese.
60 Great Victoria Street, Belfast 2. Tel: 028–9023 0115.

House of Moghul ££
Indian and European food.
60 Great Victoria Street, Belfast 2. Tel: 028–9024 3727.

Roscoff ££££
Proprietor Paul Rankin trained under master chef Albert Roux.
7 Lesley House, Shaftesbury Square, Belfast 2. Tel: 028–9033 1532. Closed: Sunday.

BELFAST – UNIVERSITY AREA

The Ashoka ££
Indian and European cuisine. Presents a food festival Sunday and Monday in summer.
363 Lisburn Road, Belfast 9. Tel: 028–9066 0362.

Chez Delbart ££
French bistro – crêpes, baked mussels.
10 Bradbury Place, Belfast 7. Tel: 028–9023 8020.

Dukes Hotel ££££
Modern French-style cooking using quality Ulster ingredients. Extensive wine list.
65 University Street, Belfast 7. Tel: 028–9023 6666.

Errigle Inn ££
Live music, roof garden.
320 Ormeau Road, Belfast 7. Tel: 028–9064 1410.

Maloney's ££
Opened in 1991. Crab en croûte, crème bavarois.
33 Malone Road, Belfast 9. Tel: 028–9068 2929. Closed: Sunday lunchtime.

New Jade Palace ££
Chinese, Cantonese and European.
717 Lisburn Road, Belfast 9. Tel: 028–9038 1116.

Saints & Scholars ££
Deep-fried Irish brie a speciality.
3 University Street, Belfast 7. Tel: 028–9032 5137.

Fresh oysters and Guinness are served in many pubs and hotels round Galway

BELFAST – EAST OF THE RIVER LAGAN
Four Winds Inn ££target
Open fires provide cosy atmosphere. Evening à la carte.
111 Newton Park, Belfast 8.
Tel: 028–9040 1957 Closed: Sunday.

BELFAST NORTH
Ben Madigan ££££
On the slopes of Cave Hill with views over city and coast. Taste of Ulster member.
Belfast Castle, Antrim Road, Belfast 15.
Tel: 028–9077 6925.
Strathmore Inn £
Steaks, grills. Salads, set lunch, à la carte.
192 Cavehill Road, Belfast 15.
Tel: 028–9039 1071.

CO ANTRIM
Adair Arms Hotel ££
Lobster soup, snails in garlic butter, à la carte.
Ballymoney Road, Ballymena.
Tel: 028–2565 3674. Last orders: 9.30pm weekdays, 7.45pm Sunday.
Angelo's Ristorante £
Cannelloni, lasagne. Unlicensed, but clients welcome to bring own wine.
3 Market Lane, Lisburn. Tel: 028–9267 2554. Closed: Sunday and Monday.
Ballyarnott House £££
Home cooking.
Oldstone Hill, Antrim. Tel: 028–2566 3292. Closes: 9pm.
Bushmills Inn £££
Gas lighting, peat fires, local products used. Speciality – River Bush salmon and Bushmills whiskey.
25 Main Street, Bushmills. Tel: 028–2073 2339.
Carriages £
Tasty grills and pizzas.

105 Main Street, Larne. Tel: 028–2827 5132. Closed: Sunday lunchtime.
Chimney Corner Hotel ££
Steaks, grills. Quick service, handy for international airport. Good à la carte menu.
630 Antrim Road, Glengormley.
Tel: 028–9084 4925.
Dionysus ££
Greek and English. Good mezze and souvlaki.
53 Eglinton Street, Portrush.
Tel: 028–7082 3855.
Ginger Tree £££
Japanese.
29 Ballyrobert Road, Ballyclare.
Tel: 028–9084 8176. Closed: Sunday.
Grouse Inn ££
Wood-panelled Bailiff's Parlour Restaurant, also grill bar. Fresh local seasonal ingredients.
2–12 Springwell Street, Ballymena.
Tel: 028–2564 5234. Closed: Sunday.
Harbour Inn £
Fresh seafood.
5 Harbour Road, Portrush. Tel: 028–7082 5047.
Hillcrest Country House ££
Close to Giant's Causeway, panoramic coastal views. Noted for seafood and sauces.
306 Whitepark Road, Bushmills.
Tel: 028–2073 1577. Open: weekends only November to April.
Jim Baker Restaurant £
Quick grills in bowling stadium.
Ballysavage Road, Parkgate, Templepatrick. Tel: 028–9443 2927. Closed: Sunday.
Londonderry Arms ££
Fresh, simple fare, home-style cooking in former coaching inn. Excellent home-made bread.
20–8 Harbour Road, Carnlough.
Tel: 028–2888 5255.

Lotus House ££
Chinese and European.
58 Bow Street, Lisburn. Tel: 028–9267 8669.

Magherabuoy House Hotel £££
View over the coast. Fresh baked salmon.
Magheraboy Road, Portrush.
Tel: 028–7082 3507.

Sleepy Hollow £££
Try pigeon breasts in red wine. Also includes an art gallery within the restaurant.
15 Kiln Road, Newtownabbey.
Tel: 028–9034 2042. Open: Wednesday to Saturday 7–9.30pm.

Templeton Hotel £££
All tastes catered for, including vegetarian. Local specialities. À la carte.
882 Antrim Road, Templepatrick.
Tel: 028–9443 2984.

The Wallace £££
Small restaurant with imaginative menu, frequently changed.
12–13 Bachelor's Walk, Lisburn.
Tel: 028–9266 5000. Closed: Sunday evening.

CO ARMAGH

Carngrove Hotel ££
Menu includes duckling, paella, à la carte.
2 Charlestown Road, Portadown.
Tel: 028–3833 9222.

Digby's & Red Grouse £
Steaks, kebabs.
53 Main Street, Killylea. Tel: 028–3756 8330. Closed: Monday and Tuesday evenings.

Drumhill House Hotel ££
Salmon, lobster.
35 Moy Road, Armagh. Tel: 028–3752 2009. Last orders: 9.30pm.

Mandarin House £
Chinese and European.
30 Scotch Street, Armagh.
Tel: 028–3752 2228.

Welcome ££
Chinese and European.
16 Bridge Street, Portadown.
Tel: 028–3833 2325.

Waterford and Limerick are well known for their fine cooked hams

CO DONEGAL

Danny Minnies £££
Pancakes a speciality. Peat fire in cosy inglenook.
Teach Killendarragh, Annagry.
Tel: 075–48201.

Errigal Restaurant £
Family, with good selection of food, keenly priced. Children's menu.
Main Street, Donegal. Tel: 073–21428.

Strand Hotel £££
Variety of home-cooked dishes served in this family-owned hotel.
Ballyliffen. Tel: 077–76107.

Water's Edge ££
The fresh-fish dishes served here are enhanced by the stunning views of Loug Swilly.
Rathmullen. Tel: 074–58182.

WATER OF LIFE

Old soldiers know that you should never volunteer for anything. Old soldiers can be wrong. Lucky (or opportunist) volunteers visiting the Old Jameson Distillery in Dublin (see page 30), or the Jameson Heritage Centre at Midleton, Co Cork (see page 70), face a rare tasting challenge – to choose their favourite from among five popular Irish whiskeys and compare them with a Scotch or Bourbon. Many people have been known to change the drinking habit of a lifetime.

Spelling apart, Irish is distinctively different from Scotch whisky. In Scotland, the malted barley which forms the basis of the spirit is dried over an open peat fire, imparting its characteristic smoky flavour. The Irish dry theirs in smoke-free kilns,

producing a clear, clean barley taste. Another difference is that Irish whiskey is distilled three times, while most similar spirits produced elsewhere are distilled only twice.

The art of distillation was discovered long ago in the Middle East – Aristotle mentioned the process in the 4th century BC – but it was first used for making perfume.

Gleaming copper pot still,
Midleton Distillery

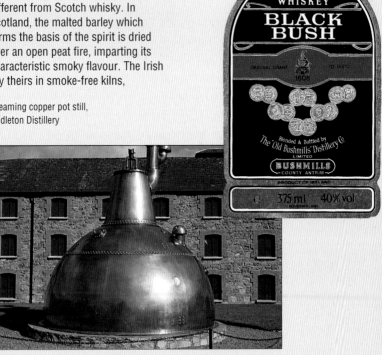

The Irish soon found a better use for it when distillation was introduced by Christian missionaries around AD600. They found a good name for the new product, too – 'Water of Life'. English soldiers serving in Ireland in the 12th century shortened the Irish phrase *Uisce Beatha* (pronounced Ish'ke Ba-ha)

to whiskey, and the word stuck.

Ireland once had more than 2,000 distilleries. Today, there are only two – at Midleton and Bushmills, Co Antrim. Bushmills, licensed since 1608, is Ireland's oldest legal distillery (see page 115). Like Midleton and the Old Jameson Distillery, it has a visitor centre.

CO DOWN

Abbey Lodge Hotel ££
Fresh oysters, crêpes.
*Belfast Road, Downpatrick. Tel: 028–4461
4511. Last orders: 9.30pm.*

Adelboden Lodge £££
Simple home cooking, including
vegetarian menu. Chef/proprietor
Margaret Waterworth is known for her
wholemeal wheaten bread.
*38 Donaghadee Road, Groomsport. Tel:
028–9146 4288. Closed: Sunday and
Monday.*

Burrendale Hotel £££
Good food and warm welcome.
*51 Castlewellan Road, Newcastle. Tel:
028–4372 2599. Lunch on Sunday only
in restaurant, bar lunches all week.*

Culloden Hotel £££
Fresh local produce used in Mitre
Restaurant – try Cream of Mitre soup.
*Bangor Road, Holywood. Tel: 028–9042
5223. Closed: Saturday lunchtime.*

Daft Eddy's £
A trip across the causeway is worthwhile
for steak, salmon, prawns.
*Sketrick Island, Whiterock, Killinchy.
Tel: 028–9754 1615. Closed: Sunday and
Monday evenings.*

Dickens £
General pub food to 9pm.
*49 High Street, Holywood. Tel: 028–9042
8439.*

Eastern Tandoori ££
Indian and European.
*16 Castle Street, Newtownards.
Tel: 028–9181 9541.*

The Gaslamp £££
Baked trout in lime and walnut sauce,
langoustines in cream and Chablis.
*47 Court Street, Newtownards. Tel:
028–9181 1225. Closed: Sunday evening.*

Granville Arms £
Hearty stews and à la carte.
Mary Street, Newry. Tel: 028–3026 1785.

Mario's £
Italian cuisine.
*65 South Promenade, Newcastle.
Tel: 028–4372 3912. Closed: Monday.*

Old Schoolhouse £££
Interesting fresh food, traditionally
cooked.
*100 Ballydrain Road, Comber.
Tel: 028–9754 1182. Closed: Monday.*

Peppercorn ££
Serves unusual local produce in sauces
made from dulse, an edible seaweed;
also Guinness and oysters.
*18 Kilmood Church Road, Killinchy.
Tel: 028–9754 1472. Open: Wednesday to
Saturday 7–10pm.*

Portaferry Hotel ££
Stuffed mussels, oysters, turbot.
*10 The Strand, Portaferry.
Tel: 028–4272 8231.*

The Red Pepper £££
Fish straight from the boats. Cheese
fondue.
*28 Main Street, Groomsport.
Tel: 028–9127 0097. Closes: 10pm
summer; reduced hours in winter.*

CO FERMANAGH

Crow's Nest £
Extensive menu. Ulster breakfast all day.
*12 High Street, Enniskillen. Tel: 028–6632
5252.*

The Hollander ££
Specialities include beef Wellington and
salmon en croûte.
*5 Main Street, Irvinestown. Tel: 028–6662
1231. Closed: Sunday lunchtime.*

Killyhevlin Hotel ££
Full à la carte menu. Moorings for
visiting cruisers.
*Dublin Road, Enniskillen. Tel: 028–6632
3481.*

Manor House Hotel £££
Elegant dining on shores of Lough Erne.
Killadeas. Tel: 028–6662 1561.

Melvin House and Bar ££
Friendly hospitality and wholesome home cooking.
1 Townhall Street, Enniskillen.
Tel: 028–6632 2040.

CO LONDONDERRY

Beech Hill Country House Hotel £££
An adventurous menu using local produce cooked nouvelle style is complemented by irresistible desserts in this fine 18th-century house, set in 13 hectares of woodland.
32 Ardmore Road, Derry. Tel: 028–7134 9279.

Brown's ££
Rack of ribs, Caesar salad, vegetarian dishes.
1–2 Bond's Hill, Derry. Tel: 028–7134 5180. Closed: Monday.

Fiolta's Bistro ££
Daily specials based on Co Londonderry products augment full menu.
4 Union Arcade, Magherafelt.
Tel: 028–7963 3522.

The Galley £
Good daytime choice. Home baking.
12a Shipquay Street, Derry.
Tel: 028–7128 8877.

Helen's ££
Chinese and European.
440 Clooney Road, Ballykelly.
Tel: 028–7776 2098.

Macduff's £££
Local country produce, game in season and Carrageen Moss, a traditional Ulster dessert.
Blackheath House, 112 Killeague Road, Blackhill, Coleraine. Tel: 028–7036 8433. No lunch served. Closed: Sunday and Monday (except July and August).

Metro Bar £
Try beef stew in Guinness.
3–4 Bank Place, Derry. Tel: 028–7126 7401. Lunches only.

Salmon Leap ££
Smoked fish, roast game in season.
53 Castleroe Road, Coleraine.
Tel: 028–7035 2992.

Trompets £
Lasagne, macaroni bake.
23 Church Street, Magherafelt.
Tel: 028–7963 2257/3522

Waterfoot Hotel and Country Club ££
Circular rooms on several levels overlooking River Foyle. Local vegetables, fish from the Foyle.
Caw Roundabout, 14 Clooney Road, Derry. Tel: 028–7134 5500.

CO MONAGHAN

Andy's Restaurant ££
Six times Ulster Pub of the Year, also National Hygiene Award winner.
Market Square, Monaghan.
Tel: 047–82277. Closed: Monday evening.

CO TYRONE

Le Curé Wine Bar £
Steaks, kebabs, vegetarian dishes.
86 Chapel Street, Cookstown.
Tel: 028–8676 2278.

Greenvale Hotel ££
Homely atmosphere in former 19th-century residence. Good à la carte menu.
57 Drum Road, Cookstown.
Tel: 028–8676 2243.

Mellon Country Inn £££
Approximately 1.5km from the Ulster-American Folk Park. Traditional food with French accent. Non-meat dishes included in extensive menu.
134 Beltany Road, Omagh.
Tel: 028–8266 1224.

Oakland Hotel at the Inn on the Park ££
Fine quality local produce used in extensive à la carte menu.
1 Moy Road, Dungannon.
Tel: 028–8772 5151.

Hotels and Accommodation

*A*ccommodation standards, closely watched by tourism authorities in the Republic and Northern Ireland, are improving constantly, and there's a good range – everything from internationally rated de luxe hotels (though not so many of these as in other countries) to simple hostels.

Both Bord Fáilte and the Northern Ireland Tourist Board run registration schemes with official grading systems, and both publish lists of accommodation with details of facilities and maximum prices. Rates must be displayed in rooms.

The two organisations have jointly developed a computerised information and reservations system to which tourist information offices throughout Ireland are linked. Under the system – known as 'Gulliver' – visitors at the Giant's Causeway, for example, are able to book accommodation in Kinsale, Co Cork, or indeed anywhere else in Ireland. Over 11,000 properties are included with accommodation ranging from hotels to farmhouses. A small charge made at the time of booking is deducted from the subsequent account.

Reservations can be made through Gulliver Ireland Reservations Direct (tel: 1800 668 668 66 from within Ireland; 00 800 668 668 66 from the UK; 011 800 668 668 66 from the US; 00 353 66 979 2082 from most other countries). Calls are free in Ireland, from the UK, US and some other countries. The service operates 8am to 8pm (to 7pm weekends) Irish time, but the hours may be extended.

Thomas Cook operate a hotel reservation desk at Dublin Airport.

HOTELS
Bord Fáilte has registered around 890 hotels with a total of some 37,000 rooms. These range from the top-class international hotels found in Dublin and other cities and major towns, to simple provincial inns. Northern Ireland has well under 150 actual hotels listed, but this does not present much of a problem in a province which can be spanned in any direction in less than three hours by car.

The Republic has a good range of accommodation in country houses – often elegant old manor houses or historic castles – with excellent, even luxurious facilities. The houses are managed in many cases by the owners themselves, who go out of their way to create a house party atmosphere. Many places have indoor pools, gyms and exercise equipment, as well as excellent sporting facilities – hunting, shooting, fishing, golf – and offer high standards of cuisine.

The Hidden Ireland, 37 Lower Baggot Street, Dublin 2 (tel: 01–662 7166) publishes a directory of country houses. *Ireland's Blue Book,* published by the Irish Country Houses and Restaurants Association, Ardbraccan Glebe, Navan, Co Meath (tel: 046–23416) lists a number of similar properties.

The Shelbourne
Generally accepted as 'the most distinguished address in Ireland' and certainly one of the world's truly grand

hotels, The Shelbourne, St Stephen's Green, Dublin, has been immortalised in literature, has witnessed dramatic moments in history and provided board and lodging for celebrities for almost 70 years.

William Makepeace Thackeray, George Moore and Oliver St John Gogarty all stayed at the hotel and wrote about it. Elizabeth Bowen was so enamoured of the place that she wrote a 200-page book about it, and James Joyce, who never actually stayed there, included it in *Two Gallants,* one of his Dubliners stories, and in his famous novel *Ulysses.*

During the Easter Rising of 1916 bullets rattled against the façade as rebels and British troops battled on St Stephen's Green. Guests were quietly moved to a room at the rear to continue afternoon tea. In 1922 the Constitution of the Irish Free State was drafted in

THOMAS COOK
Traveller's Tip

Travellers who purchase their travel tickets from a Thomas Cook network location are entitled to use the services of any other Thomas Cook network location, free of charge, to make hotel reservations (see list on pages 188–9).

the hotel. When civil war started, The Shelbourne was again in the thick of things.

The Shelbourne has been Dublin's premier hotel since 1824

GUESTHOUSES

Guesthouses are a less expensive alternative to hotels. The only difference in many cases will be in the provision of such facilities as reception areas, bars and public rooms. They consist of at least five bedrooms, often with en suite bathrooms, and guest facilities frequently include television and direct-dial telephones.

Typical town house hotel

BED AND BREAKFAST

This is probably the most popular accommodation option. B&Bs are abundant throughout the Republic, and increasing in Northern Ireland. In the Republic those approved by Bord Fáilte will display a shamrock logo.

B&Bs are officially categorised as town homes, country homes or farmhouses, but they may be no bigger than a rural bungalow with a spare bedroom. However, facilities in registered B&Bs will certainly be reasonable.

Many visitors to Ireland take pot luck with B&B accommodation, choosing a place at the end of each day's touring rather than booking ahead. But it is best not to leave it too late in the day.

FARMHOUSES

B&B apart, many farms now offer holiday accommodation on a stay-put basis. Evening meals – if the arrangement is not full board – are provided in many cases if notice is given before noon.

Peace and quiet in what may well be a very isolated location are obvious attractions, but for city dwellers at least there will be the added interest of experiencing life on the farm at first hand. Bord Fáilte is developing this concept of Green Tourism.

SELF-CATERING

Self-catering accommodation covers premises ranging from bungalows, old converted houses and semi-detached homes, to modern, purpose-designed properties built and maintained to high standards by consortia.

Members of the Irish Cottage Holiday Homes Association each manage a minimum of eight purpose-built self-catering units. All are registered by Bord Fáilte and regional tourism organisations. Standards are high (though you might be expected to provide your own towels). Many properties built recently are attractive, comfortably furnished, well equipped and have plenty of parking space. Some new properties follow traditional styles of architecture, with thatched roofs, dormer windows and stable doors.

Restored traditional cottages in lovely

These charming holiday cottages in Dunmore East provide traditional self-catering accommodation

rural locations, based on the French *gîtes* system, are available in Northern Ireland.

An option for those with grander self-catering ambitions is to rent a castle. Staff are available at some properties for those who cannot bear the thought of peeling their own potatoes or popping their own champagne corks (see Elegant Ireland address in box).

HOSTELS

An Óige, the Irish Youth Hostel Association, has 37 registered hostels, ranging from cottages and castles to former coastguard stations, schoolhouses, shooting lodges and military barracks. The hostels are available to members of the International Youth Hostels Federation (IYHF), and advance booking is advisable during the summer, especially at weekends.

Northern Ireland has nine hostels run by the Youth Hostel Association of Northern Ireland (YHANI). There is also a large number of independent hostels throughout the country. Many are members of Independent Holiday Hostel of Ireland and provide good dormitory and private accommodation at budget prices.

CAMPING

There are camping and caravan sites in each of the Republic's 26 counties, and in all six counties of Northern Ireland. The sites are officially regulated and inspected in the Republic and both tourist boards publish lists of sites (see page 179).

INFORMATION

Farmhouses
Irish Farm Holidays, 2 Michael Street, Limerick (tel: 061–400700).

Self-catering
Irish Cottage Holiday Homes Association, 4 Whitefriars, Aungier Street, Dublin (tel: 01–475 1932).
Elegant Ireland, 15 Harcourt Street, Dublin 2 (tel: 01–475 1632/1665).

Hostels
An Óige, 61 Mountjoy Street, Dublin 7 (tel: 01–830 4555).
YHANI, 22 Donegall Road, Belfast BT12 5JN (tel: 028–9032 4733).
Independent Holiday Hostels of Ireland, 57 Lower Gardiner Street, Dublin 1 (tel: 01–836 4700).

On Business

*U*ntil as recently as 20 years ago, Ireland's economy was based predominantly on agriculture. Since then, the Republic has diversified. International trading in manufactured goods, currency and commodities has contributed to a strong economy. A healthy trade surplus is equal to more than 17.5 per cent of the Gross National Product. The overall balance of payments is equivalent to 3 per cent of GNP.

The Irish have been full members of the European Community (now the European Union) since 1973, and as enthusiastic Europeans have been playing an active part in the development of the single market. As a nation, Ireland is committed to the policy of attracting new industries. It already hosts over 1,000 overseas companies, and more are showing an interest in the growing new International Services Centre under development at Dublin's Custom House Docks, as well as other locations in the Republic.

CONFERENCE FACILITIES

British companies and organisations have favoured Ireland as a conference destination for more than 30 years. Now business people from further afield are appreciating not only the facilities offered by top class hotels, but also the activities and sightseeing available near conference locations.

EDUCATION

Although the population is below four million, Ireland can boast the youngest population in Europe – around half are under 28 years of age. It is also claimed they are the best educated in Europe.

Since 1980, 20 per cent of total government expenditure has been committed to education. A third university, Dublin City University, received its charter in 1989. In the same year, Trinity College's O'Reilly Institute for Communications and Technology was opened.

Over 100,000 students are currently taking full-time, third-level courses, more than half of them in business, engineering, technology, computing and science disciplines.

Ireland has a higher graduate output per head of population than the United States. The ready availability of a well-educated young workforce is another factor which appeals to organisations considering Ireland as a base.

FLIGHTS

Dublin International Airport, 20 minutes from the city centre, has more than 160 flights a day. New York is a seven-hour flight away. Toronto, Chicago and Atlanta are within nine hours of Dublin. London is a 50-minute flight. Paris, Brussels and Amsterdam can be reached in 90 minutes. Geneva, Copenhagen, Frankfurt, Munich and Madrid are within 2 hours 30 minutes. It takes 2 hours 35 minutes to fly to Milan and 3 hours 10 minutes to Rome. There are 63 flights a day to London. (See also **First Steps – Arriving** page 18 and **Arriving** pages 178–9).

INDUSTRY

Responsible for attracting domestic and foreign manufacturing industries and financial service companies to establish themselves in Ireland, the Industrial Development Authority (IDA Ireland) has a key role in fostering and boosting the country's economy.

Backed by years of experience through 15 international and nine regional offices, IDA staff know the requirements of companies considering a base in Ireland. They respond to the need for quick decisions and a minimum of red tape.

The IDA's divisional structure – each division comprising a senior manager and a team of executives specialising in particular service and manufacturing industries – ensures that proposed projects are dealt with by the most appropriate section (see addresses in box).

MEDIA
See page 184.

TAX
Foreign companies are attracted to invest in Ireland by a variety of factors. One is a corporate tax rate of only 10 per cent – the lowest in the EU – to the year 2010, and the freedom to repatriate profits.

TELECOMMUNICATIONS
Investment of more than £5 billion during the 1980s equipped Ireland with a sophisticated digital tele-communications system, making 90 per cent of the world's telephone subscribers, from Europe to the Far East, accessible through Ireland's International Direct Dialling system.

Computer-to-computer file transfer and video conferencing are available at tariffs claimed to be among the lowest in Europe.

The new International Financial Services Centre is connected nationally

---

ADDRESSES
IDA Ireland's head office is at Wilton Park House, Wilton Place, Dublin 2 (tel: 01–603 4000, fax: 01–603 4040). Overseas addresses:
Australia Level 5, 36 Carrington Street, GPO Box 4909, Sydney, NSW 2000 (tel: 02–9262 2873, fax: 02–9262 2913).
Hong Kong 2105 Tower 2, Lippo Centre, 89 Queen's Way, Hong Kong (tel: 2845–1118, fax: 2845–9240).
UK Ireland House, 150 New Bond Street, London W1Y 9FE (tel: 020–7629 5941, fax: 020–7629 4270).
US 17th Floor, 345 Park Avenue, New York, NY 10154-0004 (tel: 212/750 4300, fax: 212/750 7357).

---

and internationally with a range of telex, digital data lines, packet switched data and voice private wires. (See also **Telephones** page 188.)

Dublin's Bank of Ireland

Practical Guide

Contents

ARRIVING

Documentation

British citizens born in the UK and travelling from Britain do not need a passport to enter the Republic or Northern Ireland, though it would be wise to carry some official form of identification – a driving licence, for example. Other EU visitors to Ireland must have a passport or suitable identity documents. Citizens from the US, Canada, Australia and New Zealand need a passport to enter either the Republic or Northern Ireland and can stay up to six months without a visa.

By air

Shannon International Airport is about 21km from Limerick. There are connecting flights to Dublin and other major centres. Taxis are located outside the main terminal building, and Bus Éireann Expressway has regular services to Limerick and other cities. The Limerick bus runs between 8am and midnight and the trip takes 40 minutes. The nearest railway station is Limerick, 2 hours 10 minutes from Dublin.

Dublin Airport is 10km from the city centre. Taxis are legion, but relatively expensive. Dublin Bus operates a half-hourly service to the city centre from 7.30am to 10.50pm daily. Journey time is about 30 minutes. There is an express bus (No 200) from Dublin to Belfast city centre (2 hours 45 minutes).

Cork Airport is well served by Bus Eireann for the 20-minute journey to Parnell Place.

Knock International Airport, Co Mayo, has an information centre and car hire facilities. There are taxis and a local bus runs to Charlestown, 11km away.

From Belfast International Airport, the regular Airbus shuttle service provides the best means of reaching Belfast, 30km away. The quickest way into Belfast from Belfast City Airport is by taxi.

The City of Derry airport at Eglinton, is served by British Airways Express with flights from Manchester and Glasgow, and is a useful gateway to Donegal and the northwest. (See **First Steps – Arriving** page 18.)

MasterCard card holders and travellers purchasing their airline ticket from any Thomas Cook Network travel locations are not charged for re-routing or re-validation of tickets (see **Thomas Cook** pages 188–9).

By sea

Ten ferry companies operate high-speed catamarans and jet-propelled craft as well as conventional vessels on ten routes between Britain and Ireland.

Using a conventional vessel, Irish Ferries takes 3¼ hours between Holyhead and Dublin, and a fast ferry takes just under 2 hours. Stena Line also operates a ferry service from Holyhead to Dublin (3¼ hours) in addition to a high-speed service from Holyhead to Dun Laoghaire (99 minutes). Both companies also run services to Rosslare – Irish Ferries from Pembroke (4 hours), Stena Line from Fishguard (3½ hours or 99 minutes).

Another operation from Wales is Swansea–Cork Ferries – 10 hours but saving a long drive to the southwest.

The quickest crossings are from Scotland. Stena Line and SeaCat Scotland operate between Stranraer and Belfast, taking between 1½ to 3 hours. P&O Euopean Ferries sails between Cairnryan and Larne in 1–2 hours.

The Argyll & Antrim Steam Packet Company sails between Campbeltown and Ballycastle in just under 3 hours.

Norse Irish Ferries takes 9½ hours between Liverpool and Belfast. Sea Containers Ferries Scotland sails from Liverpool to Dublin in just under 4 hours

while Merchant Ferries takes 7½ hours.

Irish Ferries has sailings between Rosslare and Cherbourg and Roscoff. Brittany Ferries operate services from Cork to Roscoff between April and October. (See **First Steps – Arriving** page 18.)

The Thomas Cook European Timetable has details of ferry times. (See **PUBLIC TRANSPORT** page 187.)

CAMPING AND CARAVANNING

Camping and caravan parks in the Republic are inspected and graded by Bord Fáilte and listed in its annual *Caravan & Camping Ireland* guide, which covers all 26 counties. The guide is available at local tourist information offices. Some parks are open year round, but most only from May to September.

Caravan and camping parks are categorised from 1- to 4-stars. Touring caravans and motor homes are also available for hire. Further details from the Irish Caravan and Camping Council, PO Box 4443, Dublin 2 (fax: 098–28237).

The Northern Ireland Tourist Board lists about 125 camping and caravan parks in its annual guide, *Where to Stay in Northern Ireland,* some on sites owned by the provincial Forest Service. Visitors can stop overnight at most forest locations without a reservation, though this would obviously be inadvisable in high season. A visitor's casual permit covering a period from 2 to 14 nights guarantees a space. For details contact The Forest Service, Dundonald House (Room 34), Belfast BT4 3SB (tel: 028–9065 0111, ext 456).

CLIMATE

Ireland's weather is rarely extreme. The coldest months are January and February, when average temperatures range from 4°C to 7°C. In July and August temperatures average between 14°C and 16°C. The driest area is the coastal strip near Dublin, where the average annual rainfall is less than 750mm. Rainfall in the west usually averages between 1,000mm and 1,300mm, exceeding 2,000mm in many mountainous districts. April is the driest month generally, with June the driest in many southern parts.

CONVERSION TABLES
See opposite.

CRIME
Visitors to Dublin are advised to be careful where they park and avoid leaving property visible in cars. Elsewhere, the Republic is one of the safest countries in Europe, though visitors should take the usual precautions against pickpockets or snatch-and-run thieves at large gatherings. Petty crime against the individual is comparatively rare in Northern Ireland, although petty theft and car theft is on the increase.

CUSTOMS REGULATIONS
Both the Republic and Northern Ireland operate schemes under which travellers from non-EU countries can claim a refund of Value Added Tax (VAT) on goods being taken abroad. Details are available at major stores.

DISABILITIES, TRAVELLERS WITH
Facilities for visitors with disabilities are improving. Spaces are set aside in major car parks for vehicles carrying persons with disabilities, and an Orange Badge scheme allows drivers with disabilities on both sides of the border to park for free. Bord Fáilte provides an annual guide *Carefree Journeys and Holidays* especially for people with disabilities.

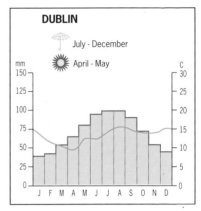

DUBLIN

☂ July - December

☀ April - May

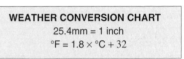

WEATHER CONVERSION CHART
25.4mm = 1 inch
°F = 1.8 × °C + 32

The National Rehabilitation Board, Access Department, 25 Clyde Road, Ballsbridge, Dublin 2 (tel: 01–608 0400; fax: 01–668 5029) publishes a county by county fact sheet and offers advice for visitors with disabilities. Wheelchairs may be hired from the Irish Wheelchair Association, Blackheath Drive, Clontarf, Dublin 3 (tel: 01–833 8241; fax: 01–833 3873). The Northern Ireland Tourist Board publishes an annual guide *Accessible Accommodation* for guidance on suitable accommodation, while further information and help is available from Disability Action, 2 Annadale Avenue, Belfast BT7 3JH (tel: 028–9049 1011; fax: 028–9049 1627).

DRIVING
Drive on the left on both sides of the border. Drivers and front-seat passengers must wear seat belts, and rear seat belts must be worn where fitted.
The Republic of Ireland has three

Conversion Table

FROM	TO	MULTIPLY BY
Inches	Centimetres	2.54
Feet	Metres	0.3048
Yards	Metres	0.9144
Miles	Kilometres	1.6090
Acres	Hectares	0.4047
Gallons	Litres	4.5460
Ounces	Grams	28.35
Pounds	Grams	453.6
Pounds	Kilograms	0.4536
Tons	Tonnes	1.0160

To convert back, for example from centimetres to inches, divide by the number in the third column.

Men's Suits

UK		36	38	40	42	44	46 48
Rest of Europe	46	48	50	52	54	56	58
US		36	38	40	42	44	46 48

Dress Sizes

UK	8	10	12	14	16	18
France	36	38	40	42	44	46
Italy	38	40	42	44	46	48
Rest of Europe	34	36	38	40	42	44
US	6	8	10	12	14	16

Men's Shirts

UK	14	14.5	15	15.5	16	16.5	17
Rest of Europe	36	37	38	39/40	41	42	43
US	14	14.5	15	15.5	16	16.5	17

Men's Shoes

UK	7	7.5	8.5		9.5	10.5	11
Rest of Europe	41	42	43		44	45	46
US	8	8.5	9.5	10.5	11.5	12

Women's Shoes

UK	4.5	5	5.5	6		6.5	7
Rest of Europe	38	38	39	39		40	41
US	6	6.5	7	7.5		8	8.5

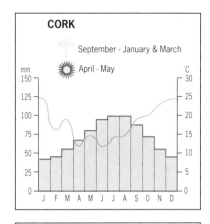

CORK

September - January & March
April - May

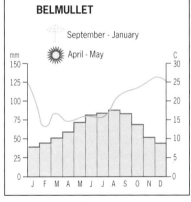

BELMULLET

September - January
April - May

road classifications: National Primary (shown with the prefix N and numbered 1 to 25), National Secondary (prefix N, numbered over 50), and Regional (prefix R).

Northern Ireland also has three road classifications: Motorways (prefix M) and A roads and B roads.

The AA has a main office at 20/21 South William Street, Dublin 2 (tel: 01–677 9950) and another office at 12 Emmet Place, Cork (tel: 021– 276922).

Breakdown

Drivers of hired cars should act according to the instructions included in their documentation. If you are driving your own vehicle and are a member of the AA or one of the AIT-affiliated driving clubs, you can call on the AA rescue service on both sides of the border.

Car hire

Major international car-hire consortia are represented throughout Ireland as well as a number of smaller local firms, who also operate under a code of conduct drawn up in the Republic by Bord Fáilte and the Car Rental Council. Car hire is cheaper in Northern Ireland than in the Republic.

Documentation

You will need a valid driving licence and, if you are bringing your own vehicle, the registration document (or a letter of authority from the vehicle owner if it is not registered in your name), plus an insurance certificate valid for either the Republic or Northern Ireland (or both).

Fuel

Fuel is cheaper in Northern Ireland. All over Ireland there are 24-hour stations.

Dublin's Ha'penny Bridge gets its name from the toll once levied on it

Insurance

Fully comprehensive cover is best, with collision damage waiver (CDW) if renting. Travel insurance does not usually cover travellers for third-party liability arising out of the use of a car; if you are hiring one, check that this is included in the hirer's insurance, or purchase a top-up policy before you travel. Check that insurance covers the Republic and Northern Ireland if you intend to cross the border.

Maximum speed limits

Republic (R), Northern Ireland (NI)
• 112kph dual carriageways and motorways (R, NI)
• 96kph country areas (NI)
• 48kph built up areas (R, NI)
• 64kph vehicles towing trailers (R)
• 88kph other roads unless otherwise indicated.

ELECTRICITY

Republic 230V AC (50 cycles).
Northern Ireland 240V AC.
Plugs everywhere are the UK standard style with three square pins; two-pin round sockets may still be found in some parts of the Republic.

EMBASSIES AND CONSULATES

Embassies in the Republic:
Australia Fitzwilton House, Wilton Terrace, Dublin 2 (tel: 01–676 1517).
Canada 65–8 St Stephen's Green, Dublin 2 (tel: 01–478 1988).
UK 29 Merrion Road, Dublin 4 (tel: 01–269 5211).
US 42 Elgin Road, Ballsbridge, Dublin 4 (tel: 01–668 8777).
Consular Offices for Northern Ireland:
Australian High Commission
Australia House, The Strand, London

WC2B 4LA (tel: 020–7379 4334).
Canadian High Commission
Macdonald House, 1 Grosvenor Square,
London W1X 0AB (tel: 020–7629 9492).
New Zealand High Commission
New Zealand House, Haymarket, London
SW1Y 4TQ (tel: 020–7930 8422).
US Consulate
Queen's House, 14 Queen Street, Belfast
BT1 6EQ (tel: 028–9032 8239).

Overseas embassies:
Australia 20 Arkana Street, Yarrulumla,
Canberra 2615, ACT. Tel: 062–273
3022/3201.
Canada Suite 1105, 130 Albert Street,
Ottowa K1P 5G4 (tel: 613/223–6281).
New Zealand 2nd Floor, Dingwall
Building, Queen Street, Auckland (tel:
09–302 2867).
UK 17 Grosvenor Place, London SW1X
7HR. Tel: 020–7235 2171.
US 2234 Massachussetts Avenue NW,
Washington DC 20008. Tel: 202/462
3939 or 3942 (other consulates in Boston,
Chicago, New York and San Francisco).

EMERGENCY TELEPHONE NUMBERS
Dial 999 for police, fire or ambulance
services in both the Republic and
Northern Ireland.
    For loss or theft of Thomas Cook
Travellers Cheques in Northern Ireland,
tel: 0800 622101 (freephone); in the
Republic, tel: 1 800 409170 (freephone).
These are 24-hour services; report your
loss within 24 hours. For loss or theft of
MasterCard cards, tel: 1 800 409170
(freephone).

HEALTH AND INSURANCE
Under an EU reciprocal arrangement,
visitors from EU countries are entitled to
medical treatment in both the Republic

and Northern Ireland, but should obtain a
qualifying form (Form E111 in the UK)
from their own National Social Security
office (or from the Post Office in the UK).
    The form should be presented to the
doctor if possible before treatment or a
consultation starts. In the Republic you
will need to make sure the doctor or
dentist is registered with the Health
Board before seeking treatment under the
reciprocal arrangement.
    UK visitors do not need to have a
Form E111 – any form of identification
proving UK-residence is acceptable.
    Visitors from non-EU countries will
need adequate medical insurance, and
even EU citizens might be advised to
seek additional cover. Medical insurance
apart, a policy should include cover
against third party liability, lost baggage
and trip cancellation. If you do undergo
treatment, make sure you keep all receipts
to present with your insurance claim.
    Travel insurance policies can be
purchased through branches of Thomas
Cook, the AA and most travel agents.
Up-to-date health advice can be obtained
from your Thomas Cook Travel
consultant.

HITCH-HIKING
In the remoter parts of Ireland, hitching
is the way the local people get around,
but they have the advantage of being
known to local drivers.
    Strangers may not be so lucky, and
might go a long time between lifts in
places where the traffic is scant at the
busiest of times. In Northern Ireland
hitch-hikers may arouse suspicion among
local people and the security forces.

LANGUAGE
English and Irish are both official
languages in the Republic, and both are

now taught in school. In the Gaeltacht areas of the west and north, Irish is likely to be the only language you will hear, and it may be the only one on the signposts. However, you will always find someone who speaks English. (See also page 185.)

LOST PROPERTY
Report serious losses – passport, credit cards, traveller's cheques – immediately. For lost passports, inform your embassy (see pages 182–3) which will be able to issue emergency documents. They may also be able to help with emergency funds if traveller's cheques are lost or stolen. (See also **Money Matters** below.)

MAPS AND GUIDES
Road maps of Ireland are freely available from car-hire companies, but for larger scale regional and town maps the best sources would be the local tourist office, where there may be a charge. Book shops throughout Ireland usually have a good stock of commercially produced maps, including those published by the Ordnance Surveys in both Northern Ireland and the Republic.

MEDIA
The Republic has four national morning newspapers: the *Irish Times, Irish Independent, The Examiner* and the tabloid *Star. The Herald* is the evening newspaper. Sunday newspapers include the *Sunday Tribune,* which carries good arts coverage, the *Sunday Business Post,* which covers the arts and international affairs as well as financial matters, the *Sunday Independent*, and the more sensational *Sunday World.* Provincial newspapers give a good insight into Irish life and reveal what is happening on the local entertainment scene.

The Republic has four television channels: RTE1, Network 2, TV3 and

TNA (the Irish-language channel). RTE stands for Radio Telefís Éireann, the state-owned broadcasting authority. UK radio and TV programmes can be received in most parts of Ireland.

In Northern Ireland the main daily newspaper is the middle of the road evening *Belfast Telegraph.* The morning papers are the Republican *Irish News* and the Loyalist *News Letter.* Ulster TV is the regional commercial channel and the Province also receives programmes from the UK mainland and the Republic. The local BBC radio station is Radio Ulster and there are a number of independent stations.

MONEY MATTERS
The Irish pound, the punt, is divided into 100 pence, with coins of 1 penny, 2 pence, 5 pence, 10 pence, 20 pence, 50 pence, £1 and £2. The most frequently used notes are £5, £10 and £20. Sterling is the currency used in Northern Ireland and the coins and notes follow the same denominations as those in the Republic. In January 1999, the Euro also became legal tender in the Republic, although currency may not be in circulation until 2002.

Banking hours in the Republic are 10am–4pm weekdays and until 5pm on Thursdays in Dublin and 5pm one day a week in other towns. Sub-branches in villages will probably be open only one or two days a week and may close for lunch. In Northern Ireland the main branches are open 9.30am–4.30pm, Monday to Friday, some now open on Saturday.

Currency and traveller's cheques can be exchanged at foreign exchange desks at the international airports on both sides of the border. Before exchanging at a bank it may pay to compare rates.

Currency can also be exchanged at some post offices and tourist information offices. Hotels will also exchange currency and traveller's cheques. Major credit cards are accepted throughout the island in hotels, large department stores and major restaurants. In Northern Ireland, MasterCard (Access) and Visa are the most readily accepted cards.

For loss or theft of MasterCard cards, tel: 1800 55 7378 (freephone). For loss or theft of Thomas Cook traveller's cheques in Northern Ireland, tel: 0800 622101 (freephone); in the Republic, tel: 00 44 1733 318950 (reverse charge). These are 24-hour services; report your loss within 24 hours.

The Thomas Cook Network travel locations (see pages 188–9) will provide emergency assistance in the event of loss or theft of MasterCard cards or Thomas Cook Travellers Cheques, and to any travellers who have purchased their travel tickets from Thomas Cook.

If you need to transfer money more quickly, you can use the *MoneyGram*^SM Money Transfer service. For more details in the UK, telephone Freephone 0800 897198.

NATIONAL HOLIDAYS

(NI) Northern Ireland only
(R) Republic only
New Year's Day 1 January
St Patrick's Day 17 March
Easter Monday
May Day first Monday in May
Spring Holiday (NI) last Monday in May
June Holiday (R) first Monday in June
Orangemen's Day (NI) 12 July
August Holiday (R) first Monday in August
Summer Holiday (NI) last Monday in August
October Holiday (R) last Monday in October
Christmas Day 25 December
St Stephen's Day (Boxing Day) 26 December.

OPENING HOURS

Shops throughout Ireland are open generally from 9am–5.30/6pm Monday to Saturday. Large shopping centres stay open until later on weekdays and may open on Sundays. Some places have early closing on one day a week. In smaller towns and rural areas in the Republic hours are more flexible, and the general

Useful Words and Phrases	Irish	*pronunciation*	English
	ceilidh	*kaylee*	traditional dance or music evening
Irish people are always pleased if visitors attempt a phrase or two in Irish. Here are a few words you may come across (along with how they are pronounced):	**Garda Siochana**	*gawdasheekawnah*	police
	tabhairne	*taw-er-nay*	pub
	slainte	*slawn-tay*	cheers
	mas e do thoil e	*maws eh duh hull eh*	please
	gura maith agat	*gurrah mah a-gut*	thank you
	la maith	*law mah*	good day
	slan	*slawn*	goodbye
	oiche mhaith	*ee-hay vah*	good night

store may also be the local pub. Pubs open in the Republic Monday to Saturday 10.30am–11pm (11.30pm summer time); Sunday 12.30–2pm and 4–11pm. Northern Ireland's pub hours are 11.30am–11pm Monday to Saturday with 30 minutes 'drinking-up' time. Most pubs are open on Sundays.

ORGANISED TOURS

There is a wide range of organised tours of Ireland, mostly by coach. There are 31 companies that are members of the Irish Incoming Tour Operators Association, which works closely with Bord Fáilte and the Northern Ireland Tourist Board. For information on guided tours in the Republic contact CIE Tours International, 35 Lower Abbey Street, Dublin (tel: 01–703 1829); for Northern Ireland contact Ulsterbus Travel Centre, Glengall Street, Belfast (tel: 028–9033 3000).

Cruising the Shannon can be an unusual way to see Ireland. River barges have been converted to give big boat stability, luxurious accommodation and haute cuisine meals.

Cruises are offered by three companies: Shannon Barge Cruises, Ogannelloe, Tuamgraney, Co Clare (tel: 0619–23044); Shannon Barge Lines, Main Street, Carrick-on-Shannon, Co Leitrim (tel: 078–20520); and Shannon River Floatels, Killaloe, Co Clare (tel: 061–376688).

The Dublin Heritage Trail bus calls at 10 specially located stops, visiting the main places of interest. There is a continuous commentary, and passengers can get on and off at their leisure. Dublin Bus, 59 Upper O'Connell Street, Dublin 1 (tel: 01–873 4222).

Another interesting city tour is the Dublin Literary Pub Crawl, in which actors guide groups round hostelries used by Beckett, Behan, Joyce and others – and the characters they created – and perform excerpts from their works (tel: 028–9045 8484).

Belfast has a narrated tour taking in the city's history and its most recent past, including the Shankhill and Falls Roads. It is operated by Citybus Tours (tel: 028–9045 8484).

PHARMACIES

Cosmetics, feminine hygiene products and photographic film are stocked, as well as prescription and non-prescription drugs and medicines. Contraceptives, now legal throughout Ireland may still be difficult to obtain in parts of the Republic. If closed, pharmacies display the address of the nearest one open.

PLACES OF WORSHIP

Catholic and Protestant churches abound, but there are few non-Christian places of worship. Synagogues are to be found in Belfast, Cork and Dublin. Mosques can be found in Dublin.

POST OFFICES

The Republic's post offices are open 9am–5.30pm Monday to Friday and 9am–1pm Saturday. Sub-post offices close at 1pm one day a week. The General Post Office in O'Connell Street, Dublin, is open 8am–8pm Monday to Saturday and 10am–6pm Sundays and public holidays. In Northern Ireland post offices are open 9am–5.30pm Monday to Friday and 9am–1pm Saturday.

PUBLIC TRANSPORT

Air

Flights from Dublin to other Irish airports are operated by Aer Lingus. The Aran Islands receive flights from Inverin, Connemara, near Galway by Aer Árann.

Bus

Bus Éireann (tel: 01–836 6111) operates a network of express routes serving most of the country. Dublin Bus–Bus Átha Cliath (tel: 01–873 4222) serves the greater Dublin area. A four-day Dublin Explorer ticket covers travel on the suburban rail network as well as all Dublin buses. Ulsterbus (tel: 028–9033 3000) runs an express link between Belfast and 21 Northern Ireland towns. Unlimited travel tickets are available. (See **First Steps – Getting Around** page 19.)

Ferry services

Licensed boat services operate from the mainland to some islands, weather permitting. The main services are: Doolin-Inishmore and Inisheer (tel: 065–74455); Baltimore–Cape Clear (tel: 028–39119); Schull–Cape Clear (tel 028–63333); Glengarriff–Garinish (tel: 027–63081); Burtonport–Arranmore (tel: 075–20532). Two important car ferries are between Ballyhack, Co Wexford and Passage East, Co Waterford (tel: 051–382480/8) and Killimer, Co Clare, and Tarbert, Co Kerry (tel: 065–53124). Crossing the Shannon estuary between Killimer and Tarbert saves 100km on the road journey.

The *Thomas Cook European Timetable* has details of rail, bus and ferry times and can be obtained from Thomas Cook branches in the UK or by telephoning (01733) 503571.

Rail

Iarnród Éireann (tel: 01–836 6222) and Northern Ireland Railways (tel: 028–9089 9411) both offer special discounted rail tickets. The Irish Rover and the Irish Explorer give unlimited rail travel for 5 out of 15 days throughout Ireland, and the Emerald Card covers island-wide bus and rail travel for various periods. (See **First Steps – Getting Around** page 19.)

Taxis

Taxis are available in major towns, at taxi stands or outside hotels, as well as at airports, main railway stations and ports. All cabs have meters, although you can negotiate fares outside main cities and airports. In Northern Ireland it is not unusual for customers to share the London-style black cabs.

SENIOR CITIZENS

Customers over 50 or 55 can obtain discounts from many car-hire companies and from some hotels and tourist attractions. Several tour operators offer special spring and autumn packages for senior citizens.

STUDENT AND YOUTH TRAVEL

Members of An Óige (Irish Youth Hostel Association) or the Youth Hostel Association of Northern Ireland (for addresses see page 175) can get discounts on some ferry crossings, and holders of a valid International Student Identity Card can buy a Travelsave Stamp which entitles them to savings on mainline rail, long distance bus and ferry services. Travelsave Stamps can be purchased from USIT, 19–21 Aston Quay, O'Connell Bridge, Dublin 2 (tel: 01–602 1600). Travel throughout Ireland is allowed with a Eurail Youthpass, available only to those under 26 who live outside Europe. The passes cover travel in 17 European countries and are available for varying periods. They can be purchased from travel agents, but must be bought before the traveller leaves home.

Dublin's DART system

TELEPHONES

Public telephones from which internal and international calls can be made are abundant everywhere. Phonecards are obtainable from post offices, newsagents and other shops. Direct dialling is cheaper than using an operator, and private phones are cheaper to use than public ones. The cheapest rates are between 6pm and 8am weekdays, weekends and public holidays. Calls made from hotel rooms are expensive.

The Thomas Cook TravelTalk card is an international pre-paid telephone card supported by 24-hour multi-lingual customer service. Available from Thomas Cook branches in the UK in £10 and £20 denominations, the card can be re-charged by calling the customer service unit and quoting your credit card number.

Northern Ireland is part of the UK telephone system, so there are no special numbers for callers from the mainland to dial. Overseas callers to Ireland must first dial their international access code:
• **Australia** 0011
• **Canada and the US** 011
• **New Zealand** 00
• **UK** (Republic only) 00.
Then dial 353 for the Republic or 44 for Northern Ireland, followed by the full

number minus the first zero of the area code. For international calls from Ireland, except Northern Ireland to Britain, dial 00 in both Northern Ireland and the Republic, followed by the country code:
• **Australia** 61
• **Canada and the US** 1
• **New Zealand** 64
• **UK** 44
Then dial the full number, omitting the first zero (does not apply to the US or Canada) of the area code.

In the Republic dial 10 for the operator, 114 for the international operator and 1190 for directory inquiries, including Northern Ireland numbers. In Northern Ireland dial 100 for the operator, 192 for directory inquiries (including numbers in the Republic), 153 for international directory inquiries and 155 for the international operator.

THOMAS COOK

The following branches and Network partners of Thomas Cook will offer emergency assistance to MasterCard cardholders and travellers who have purchased their tickets from Thomas Cook. In addition, those locations in the Republic marked ★, and all locations in Northern Ireland, offer full foreign exchange facilities and will cash Thomas Cook traveller's cheques free of commission. Opening times are 9am–5.30pm, including Saturdays (branches of J Barter, 10am–1pm Saturdays).

Republic of Ireland
Thomas Cook, 118 Grafton Street, Dublin 2★; and 51 Grafton Street, Dublin 2★.
Tommy Tobin Travel Ltd, 10 Chatham Lane, Dublin 2.
J Barter Travel Group, 92 Patrick Street,

Cork★; Unit 2, Douglas Shopping Centre, Cork; 29 West Beach, Cobh, Co Cork. Autoryan Travel, Unit 6a, Bandon Shopping Centre, Bandon, Co Cork.

Northern Ireland
Thomas Cook has both a foreign exchange bureau and a travel shop at Belfast International Airport. Other branches of Thomas Cook Travel can be found at: 11 Donegal Place, Belfast; 22–4 Lomard Street, Belfast; 39–41 Wellington Street, Ballymena; Unit 33, Bloomfield Shopping Centre, Bangor; 23 Kingsgate Street, Coleraine; 4 Bow Street, Lisburn; Unit 7, Quayside, Strand Road, Londonderry; and Unit 4, McGowan Buildings, Burroughs Place East, Portadown.

Thomas Cook's World Wide Web site, at www.thomascook.com, provides up-to-the-minute details of Thomas Cook's travel and foreign money services.

TIME
Both the Republic and Northern Ireland follow Greenwich Mean Time (GMT), but with clocks put forward one hour from late March to late October. Time difference with other countries are:
• **Australia** add 8 to 10 hours
• **Canada** subtract 3½ to 8 hours
• **New Zealand** add 12 hours
• **US** subtract 5 to 10 hours

TIPPING
Leave a tip of 10 to 15 per cent in hotels and restaurants, though some establishments include a service charge in the bill. Taxi drivers expect 10 per cent of the fare and hotel porters 50 pence a bag.

TOILETS
Public lavatories (in Irish *Fir* = Men, *Mná* = Women) are generally clean and serviceable at tourist locations.

TOURIST OFFICES
Bord Fáilte and the Northern Ireland Tourist Board both maintain offices abroad.
Bord Fáilte
Australia 5th Level, 36 Carrington Street, Sydney, NSW 2000 (tel: 02–9299 6177). Also for Northern Ireland. **New Zealand** c/o Walshe's World, Level 2, Dingwall Building, 87 Queen Street, Auckland 1 (tel: 09–379 8720). **UK** 150 New Bond Street, London W1Y 0AQ (tel: 020–7493 3201); 53 Castle Street, Belfast BT1 1GH (tel: 028–9032 7888). **US** 345 Park Avenue, New York, NY 10154 (tel: 212/418 0800).

Northern Ireland Tourist Board
Australia and New Zealand See Bord Fáilte.
Canada 2 Bloor Street West, Suite 1501, Toronto, Ontario M4W 3E2 (tel: 416/ 925 6368). **Republic of Ireland** 16 Nassau Street, Dublin 2 (tel: 01–679 1977). **UK** 24 Haymarket, London SW1Y 4DG (tel: 0541–555 250, 08701–5555 250 from 2000). **US** 551 Fifth Avenue, Suite 701, New York, NY 10176 (tel: 211/922 0101 or 800–326 0036).

There are 94 Tourist Information Offices throughout the Republic and 26 Tourist Information Centres in Northern Ireland. A third of them remain open throughout the year. Bord Fáilte's main office is at Baggot Street Bridge, Dublin 2 (tel: 01–602 4000). Northern Ireland Tourist Board's head office is at St Anne's Court, 59 North Street, Belfast BT1 1NB (tel: 028–9024 6609).

The All Ireland Information Bureau, British Visitor Centre, 1 Regent Street, London SW1Y 4NS (tel: 020–7493 3201), handles countrywide inquiries.

ACKNOWLEDGEMENTS

The Automobile Association wishes to thank the following organisations, libraries and photographers for their assistance in the preparation of this book.
AER LINGUS 18a; **BORD FAILTE** 32, 41, 42, 47, 60, 62, 63, 65a, 65b, 68a, 71b, 91, 138, 153; **INTERNATIONAL PHOTOBANK**; **THE SLIDE FILE** 128; **WATERFORD CRYSTAL** 67.
The remaining photographs are held in the AA PHOTO LIBRARY with contributions from:
L BLAKE 50, 69a, 83, 157. J BLANDFORD 5, 16, 23, 67, 71a, 79, 104b, 123, 124, 125, 131, 155. D FORSS 39a, 48/9, 72, 76, 82. CHRIS HILL 1, 12, 17, 21, 28, 80, 84, 85, 87a, 87b, 88, 90, 93, 95, 98, 101, 102, 107, 110, 112, 113, 114, 115, 117, 129, 130, 136b, 139, 144, 145, 149, 150, 151, 152, 154a, 154b, 159, 160, 165, 167. STEFFAN HILL 11b, 18b, 19b, 20, 22a, 22b, 29c, 37b, 70, 73, 74, 75, 105a, 126, 127, 133b, 136a, 137b, 147a, 168. J JENNINGS 2, 69b, 104a, 108a, 108b. G MUNDAY 10, 14, 15, 24, 26a, 26b, 28/9, 30, 33, 34, 38, 40, 45, 57, 100, 103, 104/5, 105b, 106, 109, 122, 147b. MICHAEL SHORT 4, 6, 13, 19a, 27, 29b, 35b, 36, 36/7, 37a, 37c, 39b, 44, 46, 48a, 51, 52, 53, 54, 55, 64, 66, 86, 137a, 142, 142/3, 143a, 143b, 146a, 146b, 173, 174, 177, 175, 182, 188. W VOYSEY 9, 35a, 132, 133a, 133b. P ZOELLER 29a, 68b.

CONTRIBUTORS
Series adviser: Melissa Shales   **Copy editor**: Sheila Hawkins   **Verifier**: Colin Follett
Indexer: Marie Lorimer